PRA
EMPO\

"*Empower Trip* provides teens   ...ul and tangible tools they can use right away to navigate the ups and downs of life, starting from adolescence and lasting through the decades that follow. With this book, John Henry and his co-authors have given teens a roadmap for a successful life, starting with their mental and emotional states and rippling out to their diet, exercise, social, and career choices. I want to give *Empower Trip* to every teenager I know!"

–Kelly A. Turner, PhD, NY Times bestselling author
of *Radical Remission* and *Radical Hope*

"This book will provide the tools for your teen to boost their confidence, build a positive self-image and practice self-love as they face daily challenges through their journey of life. The short stories and activities that begin each chapter, along with the affirmation statements, make this book relevant and thought-provoking. Readers will reflect on the importance of being mindful when dealing with challenges and how their actions will help them gain self-control and instill the courage to move forward. When reading this book, it truly feels like you are on an adventure and that your life can be filled with endless possibilities."

–Rose Acerra, past president, New Jersey PTA and
vice president of advocacy, National PTA

"I am thrilled about this book! It captures astutely the need of teenagers today. The tools are not only perfectly varied and comprehensive, but also practical, creative, fun and effective. After just my first read, and I can't wait to read the book again, I am already thinking of several teenagers I know need this book! In fact, from my 30 plus years working with teenagers, I know for a fact that they have been waiting for it! It will be an ongoing pleasure for me to recommend this collection of visionary exercises to many, many people for years to come."

–Dr. Regalena Melrose, trauma specialist, author, educator, trainer

"The road to empowerment is no small trip. For teens facing new experiences and increasing responsibility, developing personal empowerment is a fundamental process not often taught in classrooms. Fortunately, Henry and co-authors have provided a guide packed with activities to build self-care skills that can last a lifetime. Based on extensive personal and professional experiences and expertise, the authors display how growing your inner star power is not only empowering, but also a lot of fun. I highly recommend this book for teens, young adults, and educators or anyone who wants more inner star power!"

–Dr. Michelle D'Abundo, PhD, MSH, CHES, ELI-MP,
Associate Professor at Seton Hall University

"Empower Trip is packed full of invaluable lessons for teens on discovering and developing their unique identity and abilities. Every page shines a brilliant light on why teens are capable of greatness, and how the world needs yours!"

–Jonathan Catherman sociologist, educator,
international bestselling author

"Empower Trip is a great resource for developing and improving social and emotional learning in schools. There are tips for parents, teachers and for the students to manage their own well-being. Using current pop culture references, it presents strategies and skills students need to properly manage their social and emotional readiness for learning."

–Dr. Henry Cram, former New Jersey and New York
school superintendent, president emeritus of the
Middle States Association, published author

"This is a well-thought-out book students and teachers can use as an individual resource or class resource for social-emotional and holistic well-being. The range of topics explored includes know yourself, have courage, forgiveness, and eat for wellness with a structure of an affirmation, a sample story, and possible ways to address the concerns. For youth and grown-ups who can easily identify with the themes, it creates self-awareness and ways to feel good about yourself. Teachers and adults that work with children can now have a comprehensive resource that gives students the tools for their path, and a holistic approach to their overall well-being. The stories are so common and close to home for many students so they won't feel isolated and will find a path of connections to address life's journey as we know it."

–Joaquin Vega, principal of the Bronx International High School

"This beautifully written book invites a new generation to start reading self-help books. Deeply engaging, heartfelt, and thoughtful for teenagers who need the authors' wisdom and support more than ever. *Empower Trip* teaches the readers how to become well-rounded, well balanced, happy, and healthy adults. The examples in each chapter are very relatable and inspirational. The tools this book offers are immensely helpful. A brilliant handbook for every generation."

–Katalin Berland, PhD in Child Psychology, former teacher, counselor, parent consultant

"As the owner of a wellness center and a mother, I appreciate the healing power of this book. Kids don't always learn how to empower themselves at home or at school and *Empower Trip* creates that possibility for them! It provides a plethora of relatable stories, tools, and activities for our youth to feel powerful and worthy, to get to know who they are, find confidence and be what all parents want, happy."

–Tracy Cleary, owner of Pure and Simple Health and Osteostrong, New York

"*Empower Trip* is an excellent read for young adults and others, that will help them learn how to think, rather than what to think.

The book is filled with strategies to support the development of the power of belief, reframing thoughts, expanding one's comfort zone, **and the use** of self-talk. In a world where love is seen less and less, the importance of learning about self-love is emphasized. Many easy-to-do exercises are provided to make the learning experiences interesting and fun. Children are our future, and this book helps them to expand their vision and realize their power."

–Jim Cullum, certified hypnotherapist, stress management instructor, author of *Let Me Show You How I Love You*

"It is my honor to stand beside these incredible authors and their stories, as well as the wisdom and community of empowerment in these pages. Do yourself, your children, your grandchildren, and their children a favor and start a book club with this in hand and in heart. Many books have been written about self-love, self-respect, and self-awareness, but this one will most assuredly hold a special place in history. To learn to stand in your own confidence and self-worth, regardless of the external circumstances is a lesson that reaches far beyond this lifetime."

–Dr. Renee Boccio, holistic chiropractor, functional medicine practitioner, wellness advocate

EMPOWER TRIP

A Teen's Guide to Finding Your
Inner Star Power

John Henry, Dana Hice DePugh, Kim Weiler

Empower Trip, LLP

Disclaimer
This book is intended for students who may find the information useful and helpful. If there are challenges that impact emotional well-being, academic success, or physical health, please see an adult you trust to help you find competent medical, educational, or psychological professionals. While reasonable efforts have been made to ensure the accuracy and helpfulness of this book, the authors are educational professionals, not medical doctors, psychologists, psychiatrists, mental health workers, social workers, or any type of medical or healthcare professionals.

Published by
Empower Trip LLP.
www.empowertrip.org
4626 Waltmoor Road
Wilmington, NC 28409

Library of Congress Control Number: 2023918509
Paperback ISBN: 979-8-9892094-0-8
Ebook ISBN: 979-8-9892094-1-5

Cover design by Dana Hice DePugh
Interior design by Dana Hice DePugh
Edited by The Reading List

This book is dedicated to our youth, our next generation of leaders. Working on empowering yourself requires courage, and you are truly brave.

CONTENTS

INTRODUCTION

On any given night, you can look up at the stars and see them sparkling in the sky. Although they are far away, they're energetic and radiant. Stars are a powerful source of light, and tools like telescopes can magnify their beauty and brightness.

You have the same kind of power inside of you.

You too have the ability to shine and sparkle magnificently.

You have the opportunity to share your light and your gifts with others.

And just like a telescope can help a star's light be seen more easily by someone observing it, we hope that by reading this book and using the tools you find here, you'll find ways to let your inner starlight shine.

Here's one important way you're different from a star: As you travel on your path toward the future, you have control over where you are going and how you get there. This book is designed to empower you to create a life you love and to arrive at a better understanding of yourself and others. "Empowering" someone means making them stronger and more confident, and even though things may feel challenging sometimes, you have the power to focus on what really matters, to feel worthy, and to chart your path through life.

As you explore this book, you will learn to identify your strengths, improve your interactions with others, and love who you really are. Each chapter starts out and ends with a quote and an affirmation to inspire you. You will find a story about someone who encountered obstacles on their path and found ways to overcome them. Following each story is a brief explanation of why this topic is important to address on your empower trip. Next are tools you will use to empower yourself and activities you can choose from to facilitate your personal growth. You can do these activities alone or with friends, family, or adults from your school.

You can work through the book from start to finish, chapter by chapter, or choose a topic that interests you and explore the book in the order you prefer.

Tools are for fixing, altering, building, creating, and maintaining things. The chapters in this book are like the drawers in a toolbox—they can be opened whenever you need a specific tool for a specific job. Each drawer, or chapter, represents an emotion you may wish to work through and is filled with tools to help you. As you use them, you'll start to build positive, healthy habits. Your journey toward empowerment will take time, but small steps each day will build awareness and eventually create change. You may even see an opportunity to share what you've learned with someone you care about or perhaps a stranger in need.

You may be going through something right now in your life that you keep *hoping* will change or simply go away. Yes, hope can be inspirational, but actual *action* is what yields results. You can't hope that things will get better in your life or hope an uncomfortable situation will change. Hoping is not really a strategy. Some of the first steps to solving your problems include learning all you can about the situation, planning to do something, and then taking action. Use the tools in this book, instead of simply hoping, as the first step in creating your action plan.

You will confront obstacles along the pathway of your life's journey, but know that these obstacles point the way to your future. When an obstacle stands in your way, you can choose to face it head on and learn from it instead of letting it bring you down. Every obstacle is an opportunity for personal growth.

If you don't play a role in designing your life the way you want it, you might find yourself working toward someone else's goals for you. You need to be the driver of the bus, not the passenger, on your empower trip. You may make mistakes on this journey toward empowerment, and that is okay. You can look to friends and family for support when needed, but know that the power lies within you. Yes, sometimes you have to learn by doing, and it does not have to be the hard way. Know that whatever feelings you are experiencing, they're normal and a part of growing. You are and always will be a shining light in this world.

As you build good habits and start to reach for some of the tools we'll offer you in the chapters ahead when you need them, this book will help you change your thoughts. It will help transform them from limiting beliefs about yourself to a powerful knowing that reflects how wonderful you really are. Self-empowerment is a great first step, and you will be surprised at how life-changing believing in yourself can be. How many times have you thought, *I'm not good enough* or *I'm not pretty enough or strong enough* or *I'm not talented enough*? Positive change will come to you when you shift your words and refocus your thoughts to *I am good enough*, *I am pretty*, *I am strong*, *I am talented.* Believing in yourself will help you design and create a life you deserve.

In this book, we will identify ways to use tools such as affirmations, meditations, visualizations, and setting intentions. Many of these activities require you to do some thinking, while others are hands-on and fun, where you do some creating. Working your way through the strategies will focus and clarify your thoughts, helping you accomplish your goals. At the beginning and end of each chapter, you will find affirmations. Positive affirmations are beneficial words and statements that, when used consistently, can help you believe something good that eventually becomes your reality. They change negative words and thinking into positive words and thoughts. Affirmations can help change your future by motivating you to believe in yourself and take action. Positive affirmations can increase your self-confidence by reminding you that you have an inner light, and you can shine.

Many people who achieve success set goals and positive intentions. We encourage you to set some goals for yourself as well. Please remember, though, that not every goal can be accomplished alone. It is important to surround yourself with others who are good for you, support you, and have your back. In other words, who do you want to come along with you on your journey to success and happiness? Trust your gut if someone who's riding along with you is distracting you from your dreams. If someone is hindering your travels, ask them to step out of the way. The tools in this book will help you learn to surround yourself with supportive people. Seek out teachers, advisors, parents, and trusted friends who can help you along the way.

Self-awareness is one of the qualities you will be developing when you set out on this pathway to empower yourself. This simply means that you will be getting to know yourself better. You are an amazing and special person, and you have some wonderful qualities that you should know about. It is valuable for you to identify, for example, that you are an exceptional artist, a loyal friend, or a spectacular student in science class. It is equally important to identify the parts of yourself that you would like to accept or work on improving. For example, you may feel that dancing is simply not your thing. If you don't enjoy dancing and don't want to improve your dancing, you can simply choose to say that dancing is not your thing. If you do want to improve your dancing, you can take lessons and practice, and it's quite likely your dancing will improve!

The goal of learning more about yourself is to learn to love yourself. *Self-love* is the process of accepting both your positive and negative qualities. If you don't love yourself, it may be difficult for you to achieve your goals. Self-love is at the core of your personal empowerment and growth.

Are you ready for an adventure? We invite you to gather your courage and read on. In traveling these pages, may you feel powerful and worthy. May you fall in love with your life—a life of endless possibilities. May the power be with you as you discover your inner star and let it shine.

PART ONE: ALL ABOUT YOU

Chapter 1: Know Yourself

Awareness is the greatest agent for change.
—Eckhart Tolle

Affirmation: Every day there is something new and amazing to learn about myself.

Luis's Story

Luis was dreading his cousin's wedding, which was about a month away. He loved his cousin, and her boyfriend was cool. He was happy for them. His problem? Luis knew all the wedding guests would be out on the dancefloor at the reception, and he couldn't dance. He'd tried plenty of times. He'd turned the radio on really loud and tried to get some groove going in his room when no one was looking. He'd asked his sister to help him, and she'd giggled and said something about two left feet. He'd watched videos online and tried to copy the moves, but after hours practicing, he still didn't feel great about his dancing.

So, Luis decided to ask his Uncle Johnny, who was catering the wedding, if he needed any help in the kitchen. Luis loved to cook. He made breakfast for his family every weekend, and even his sister said his food was good! Uncle Johnny happily took Luis up on his offer. On the day of the wedding, Luis worked next to his uncle, and they put out a ton of food. Although Luis didn't dance at the wedding, he spent his time in the kitchen with his uncle doing what he loved and what he was good at. People were happy. Luis was happy. It turned out to be the best party he ever attended.

Why You Should Get to Know Yourself

Knowing yourself is called *self-awareness*. While becoming fully self-aware can be a lifelong process, one of the first steps is learning about your strengths and weaknesses. Uncovering what you like and what you enjoy helps you to become more attuned to yourself. Identifying the areas of yourself you would like to improve and the things that challenge you is also a part of self-awareness. As you slowly get to know who you are and how you feel about the world around you, you may naturally become more confident about how you fit in.

All of us struggle to be our authentic selves at times because it's often easier to try to belong. Daring to show that you are different, and offering others your true self, can be difficult when you want to be liked. But trust us: you can still be liked for being who you truly are! Learning more about yourself can help you trust your intuition and become a better decision-maker. When you understand your emotions and your perspectives, you understand what you truly want, and you make better decisions for yourself. Spending time doing the things you enjoy and focusing on what's important to you will also help you lead a happier life. When you know yourself, you are more able to set appropriate goals for yourself.

Getting to Know Your Inner Star

Me Date

A Me Date is a date that you go on solo. You get to do whatever it is *you* want to do on a Me Date. If you like sitting in the park and watching the people, do it. If you want to watch *Freaky Friday* for the fifteenth time, curl up on the couch and go for it! If music is your thing, listen to your favorite songs, and dance around the room like no one is watching with . . . yourself. Yes, you! You are great company! You can date yourself for the entire evening, or you can have a mini-date that lasts for as little as ten minutes. Have fun. Getting to know yourself on a Me Date is a blast!

IM Collage

No, this IM is not an instant message, although you probably have a ton of those. This IM stands for "I am." You are going to make a collage out of pictures and/or words. The pictures or words should represent you and some of the things you like. If you have a bunch of old magazines sitting around your house, you can cut out images and text that express who you are.

Glue these pictures and words on a piece of paper or cardboard and cover every inch. Don't leave any bare space. If you prefer to make your collage online, there are some great websites to help you. Simply search the internet for "free collage maker" and have some fun. When you're done, print your collage and put it somewhere visible, so you can remind yourself of all the wonderful things there are to like about you!

Getting to Know You

Another way to get to know yourself better is through free self-assessments and self-evaluations. The web is filled with various questionnaires. You can learn about your likes, dislikes, aspirations, fears, abilities, and challenges. The best thing about these little quizzes is that you can't fail! Taking a self-assessment can help you understand yourself and your emotions better. You can find some good ones by searching online. A few of our favorites are Myers-Briggs, 16 Personalities, Personality Academy, and Truity. It can be fun to take these tests with friends and family and share your results with each other. Be sure to avoid sharing your personal information (such as your address, phone number, etc.) and follow your family's and school's internet safety practices when doing these surveys or inventories.

Be Your Own Pen Pal

Pen pals are people who write to each other, and being your own pen pal is a great way to learn more about yourself. Write a letter to yourself, introducing yourself to you! Tell yourself about all the positive qualities you have. Tell yourself about your likes and dislikes. Write about your goals for your future and what makes you happy. Put the letter somewhere safe, and read it once a month. It's fun to see if anything has changed and how you grow and evolve.

Do New and Do Now

For one week, try to do something new each day. This can be something simple, like eating different foods, listening to a new artist, wearing your hair in a different style, or doing a yoga video before school. Start small and stay safe! (Avoid anything that could be dangerous.) After you have done the new thing, think about whether you enjoyed it. If it's something you enjoyed, you'll probably want to do it again. Exploring your likes and dislikes can be exciting and super fun.

Me Meme

We all become aware of various aspects of our personality as each day passes. We have both strengths and weaknesses, and it's important to be able to identify these qualities. Think about a strength or weakness, and begin designing your own personal meme. A meme is an image, saying, video, or song that goes viral. Think about what pictures and symbols might represent you best. Your meme can be inspiring, like a certain affirmation you find meaningful. Your meme could also be humorous and make light of a certain characteristic of your life. You can put "meme maker" into your search bar to find websites to help you make your meme. Keep your meme appropriate and respectful. You don't have to post it on social media, but you can certainly try to make it go viral if you like!

Self-Awareness Superhero

Decide on a personal quality that you really like about yourself —for example, being a loyal friend, being confident, having a good sense of humor, or being smart. Once you pick a quality, design a character whose superpower is this wonderful quality. Create a comic or storyboard that shows the superpower in action. This can be done using whatever material you choose (digital illustrator, markers, crayons, etc.). For example, if you decide your best quality is kindness, you might draw a superhero flying in the sky, spreading kindness through rays of light to others on the planet. Display this drawing somewhere you can see it to strengthen your awareness of this beautiful quality.

Personal PSA

A public service announcement (PSA) is a message that gives people in a community information that can help them in some way. It's a short message, about a minute long, intended to make the public aware of something. Think about something you do that helps others. For example, maybe you walk your friend's younger sibling home from the bus stop to make sure they are safe. Create a short video sharing what you do and how it helps, while encouraging others to do the same. Imagine your personal PSA reaching people of all ages in your community, so they too can help others. Keep this video to remind yourself of all the positive things you do to help others, and feel free to share it with your family or friends if you wish.

Affirmation: I am learning about myself, and I appreciate all of my beautiful qualities.

Knowing yourself is the beginning of all wisdom.
—Aristotle

Chapter 2: Love Yourself

Love yourself first and everything else falls into line.
—Lucille Ball

Affirmation: I love and accept all of me.

Kim's Story

Kim went to Cancun, Mexico, on spring break with a group of friends. She had so much fun getting ready to go out! She went dancing all night and lay on the beach all day. It was so freeing being away with friends for the very first time . . . until the day they were hanging out by the pool, and she noticed that her legs were covered in small, red, scaly spots. The sun was blazing, and the spots were lobster red. A few friends asked about the spots, and Kim was *mortified.* She managed to act as if it wasn't a big deal and quickly jumped into the pool.

Meanwhile, inside she was *dying* of embarrassment! All her friends were feeling so good in their skin, so confident. She was so envious! She had a skin condition called psoriasis, which produced red inflamed spots on her skin that were itchy and uncomfortable. She was beyond self-conscious and was upset with the timing of the outbreak. She spent the rest of the trip sweating in jeans because she didn't want anyone to see the spots.

When she returned home from that trip, the psoriasis affected everything she did, every decision she made, every outfit she wore. She lied to friends, to the boy she dated, and worst of all to herself. She kept telling herself that she wasn't enough, she was worthless, and she was ugly. One day, she found herself on the bathroom floor ugly crying and gasping for breath. Her sister encouraged her to find ways to love and accept herself with or without spots on her skin.

This thought was so new to Kim. Love herself with a skin disease? How the heck could she do that? Kim's sister told her how beautiful she was on the inside, despite how she felt on the outside. She reminded Kim that the spots were temporary, and this helped Kim start her journey of self-acceptance. That powerful moment was the beginning of finding love for herself. She had always looked to the outside world for love, now she was learning to find it inside.

Why You Should Love Yourself

Loving yourself is such an interesting concept, because it is not something that can be defined easily or in a few words. Loving yourself is something we work to achieve. Real self-love means unconditionally loving yourself every minute of every day, with the good, the bad, and the ugly! When you love yourself, it enables you to gain confidence. Self-love helps you feel more willing to take risks, fully express yourself, and not repress any of your emotions. You can take responsibility for your actions and try new things. Loving yourself also strengthens your immune system, increases your self-esteem, and allows you to feel more positive emotions. *This* is the path to success and chasing your dreams. Practicing self-love will help you transform any negative story your mind might be telling you. For example, in the story above, Kim decided to change her negative thoughts of shame to thoughts of love for herself. This shift in thinking helped her create a self-love practice, and that changed her life for the better.

Learning to Love Your Inner Star

Kind Self-Talk

Consider something about yourself that makes you uncomfortable. It could be something physical like your skin, as in the case of Kim from our story, or it could be a habit like biting your nails. Say something kind and loving about that specific thing to yourself, instead of focusing on the negative. For example, Kim could instead say to her skin, *I know you are healing, and I appreciate that. You are beautiful and I love you.* For biting your nails, you could say something to yourself like *I am in control of my body. I have the power to keep my nails out of my mouth. I love my nails and enjoy letting them grow.*

Talking to yourself might feel awkward at first, but with practice over time, it will start to feel good. You may find that you won't want to miss a day of talking to yourself because being kind to yourself will feel so good. Commit to a week, and continue to say your kind, loving words to yourself. Consider how you feel after the first week. For the second week, pick a different issue or topic and do this again. Consider making this a regular practice in the future. Regularly using kind self-talk can train your mind to be kinder and more loving to you.

Joy List

What brings you joy? Write this question on a piece of paper. Then make a list of everything you can think of that brings you joy, big or small. Some examples may include enjoying healthy smoothies, hugging a parent, going for a walk, petting your dog, or hanging out with friends. Hang this list somewhere you can see it, and add to it as often as you like. Refer to this list regularly, and choose one thing to do to help you feel good and bring you more joy.

Fortune Finds

Most of us have had a fortune cookie at one time in our lives. This little cookie contains a small piece of paper with a prediction for the future written on it. If you find yourself worrying a lot or running through negative scenarios in your mind, here's a way to turn those words into a positive fortune for your future. For example, if you're worried about having what you need in the future, write a fortune that says something like *No need to worry! You will always have everything you need!* If you worry about meeting your goals, you might write something like *You will always be successful and confident.*

If you have trouble with this activity, you can search the internet for "fortune cookie sayings" and pick some that inspire you. Write your fortunes on small strips of paper or type them up and print them out. Place the fortunes around your house, at the bottom of your nightstand drawer, in the pantry, etc. When you find them later, reread them as many times as you like. Enjoy these positive messages and predictions for your future!

Bank!

When we think about the word *valuable*, we often associate it with the word *money*. In thinking deeply about this word, consider a different definition, one that has to do with being useful or helpful to others. Sometimes we do things in our daily lives that help others, and we don't even realize it. Maybe you have loaded the dishwasher for your mom and cleaned out the sink so she doesn't have to do it when she comes home from a long day at work. Maybe you saved a seat on the bus for a friend. We do little things every day that make a difference in the lives of others. If you have an old piggy bank, you can use it for this activity. Otherwise, you can make your own bank using an old shoe or shipping box. Just carefully cut a small hole in the top. You can decorate it using positive words that remind you how useful and helpful you really are! At the end of each day, write down the things you have done that are helpful to others and deposit them in your bank. At the end of the week, reread and count your deposits. How many do you have? How many do you have at the end of the month? You do valuable things every day, and your positive qualities really do make you rich!

Good Graffiti

Consider the most important thing you want to work on and what you need to remind yourself about more often. Using a positive word or words, complete the following sentence: *I am* _____. You can use words like *intelligent*, *a positive influence*, *kind*, or *healthy* to complete this sentence. Use markers or colored pens and draw out your completed sentence on a piece of paper that can be covered in clear tape, and affix it to something you'll see every day. Your orange juice glass might have the message *I am in control* if paying attention in school is challenging for you. Your toothpaste tube might have the message *I am happy for others* if you struggle with jealousy. Say the message to yourself whenever you see the item, and try to repeat it throughout the day to keep yourself on the right track. If your parents or guardians are okay with it, you can also write your message directly onto an item in your house.

Cast a Spell

For this activity, you will create a personal affirmative "spell" to help yourself accomplish something you need to work on. Sit and think of one word that describes a goal you have for yourself. The word should describe a positive quality like *HAPPY*, *CONFIDENT*, or *PEACEFUL*. Spell the word out using one letter from the word on each line. (You may have done an acrostic at school before.) Each letter will begin a sentence that describes the magic this creates in your life. So, your spell could look like the following:

> **H**onor all the hard work and effort I have put into my daily activities.
> **A**ppreciate the people who take care of me and help me.
> **P**ay better attention to all my small accomplishments.
> **P**ut time aside during my day to do things I enjoy.
> **Y**oga and exercise are things that help keep me joyful and calm.

Post your spell somewhere that will remind you to keep casting it. This can be used as a prompt when you need a boost to help keep you on track.

Theme Song

A theme song is a musical piece in a movie or video game that plays at the beginning and sets the tone for the entire story. Research songs with positive messages on Spotify, YouTube, Apple Music, or Vimeo, and pick a theme song for yourself that sets the tone for where you aspire to be in your life. Some great theme songs include Kelly Clarkson's "Stronger," Journey's "Don't Stop Believing," and Alicia Keys's "This Girl Is on Fire." Play the song whenever you need a lift or you want to be inspired to remember everything great about yourself. You can also set your phone's ring tone to play the song.

Cheers to You

Cheerleaders are individuals who chant slogans of encouragement and motivation, sometimes with pom-poms in hand. You can be a cheerleader for yourself to showcase your love for you! Use a traditional cheer or a more contemporary one like a hip-hop song. Search the internet for a cheer that inspires you or make your own. Say the cheer out loud to yourself while looking in the mirror. If you have a pom-pom, or can find one at a reasonable price, you can use that while cheering for yourself.

You can also make your own pom-pom with an old pen or pencil, some tape, a pair of scissors, and some paper towels. Wrap three or four paper towels around the point of the pen or pencil and use the tape to fasten it to the surface. Use the scissors to cut the paper towels vertically in the direction of the eraser or top of the pen up to where the tape ends, cutting each layer separately and in different spots. When you have completed cutting, push back the layers to reveal your pom-pom. You can laugh, have fun, and get silly with your pom-pom any time to cheer something wonderful about yourself. You can keep it on your desk at home and give yourself a shake when you accomplish something great or need some encouragement.

You Movie

If you have access to an app such as iMovie, Adobe Rush, or Funimate, you can create a video for yourself that includes inspirational photos and affirmative sayings. You can also include music. Search online for affirmations about self-love. Write down ten to twenty that make you feel good. Record yourself saying the affirmations on the app where you are constructing the video. Search for photos that inspire you and upload them into the video app. Choose uplifting music to add to your video. Try to keep your video's run time between thirty seconds and one minute, and play it for yourself each day. Playing your video daily can help you to feel inspired and uplifted. This can also be something you create for a friend, to help them realize the wonderful things about themselves.

Affirmation: I am choosing to love myself every day.

*Love yourself first because that's who you'll
be spending the rest of your life with.*
—Unknown

Chapter 3: Believe in Yourself

Positive belief in yourself will give you the energy needed to conquer the world and this belief is the power behind all creation.
—Stephen Richards

Affirmation: I believe that no obstacle can stand in the way of what I want to accomplish.

Juanita's Story

As the biggest basketball game of the season approached, Juanita began to doubt that her team would win. The other team was undefeated and had some of the top players, who were very intimidating. She was captain of the team and had the opportunity to encourage the other girls to believe they could win. She was full of anxiety and knew her teammates were feeling that energy from her. Her coach could see the fear in their eyes, so he encouraged them to watch the movie *Miracle*.

It's about the USA Olympic hockey team in the 1980s that eventually played against the Russian team. The Russian team was older and more experienced. The American team was good, but they lacked the belief that they could win. Their coach was a pivotal factor in preparing them mentally and physically for the game. The power of belief and hope the coach instilled in them had a miraculous impact on the team's mindset and performance.

Juanita and the girls were inspired by seeing how others overcame obstacles when faced with adversity. They felt motivated to work harder at practice and slowly began to erase the thoughts of losing. They texted each other empowering quotes and hung positive affirmations in the locker room, such as *We Got*

This, *We Are Worthy*, *We Are Fearless*, and *Anything Is Possible*. They started to believe they could win.

When the day of the big game came, it was close, but they were doing great. There were only a few seconds left, and Juanita's team was down by one point. Juanita had the ball. She grounded herself with confidence, whispered to herself "I got this," and took the last shot from about fifteen feet out. The shot went in, and the team was victorious. Because they changed their thinking from negative to positive and practiced hard, the results they wanted—and got—were impacted by the process of believing.

Why You Should Believe in Yourself

Believing that something is possible is the first step in making it a reality. If you believe something positive can happen, you can construct a plan to get to your goal. Believing in yourself can be empowering. Once you construct your plan, you can connect the power of believing to the physical or mental steps you need to take. If you strive to do anything in your life but don't truly believe it is possible, it's not likely to happen. You can train your mind to believe that you are surrounded by possibility. Practicing positive thinking, rather than allowing limiting beliefs to take over your mind, can allow you to live with limitless possibilities. Negative beliefs will not let the power of success grow. Keep in mind that believing something positive will happen is not a guarantee that it *will* happen, but it certainly helps.

An example of the power of belief can be found in Harvard researcher Henry K. Beecher's *placebo effect.* The placebo effect has been observed in research experiments where subjects are given pills that have no medicine in them at all—placeboes—and are told the pills may help them. A percentage of people in these studies actually do end up getting better, even though they did not receive medication. They believed they would get better, and they did.

You can often change the results of a situation with the belief system you create. Olympic athletes are a good example of this because many of them practice believing by visualizing. They will see themselves living out their dreams and use their imagination to make their vision a reality. They will imagine their Olympic event as if it's happening, one thought at a time, going over every move in their minds. They see the outcome they want as if it's already happened and do not believe failure is an option. They visualize and believe in success. We are what we believe. When we change our beliefs, we change our behaviors, and when we change our behaviors, we can change our lives.

Ways to Believe in Your Inner Star Power

Red Light, Green Light

As you know, when you are driving and you see a red light, you stop, and when you see a green light, you go. Red lights keep you from getting where you need to go, and green lights let you move forward on your path. Your words can be a little like red lights at times; they can keep you from going where you need to go. For example, if you say, *I will never pass my algebra test*, you are putting a big red light in front of passing your algebra test. Give yourself a green light instead, and say something like *I believe if I study and go for extra help, I will pass my algebra test.*

Red and green markers, pens, or crayons will work best for this activity. Fold a piece of paper in half. In red, write something on one side of the page that is negative and keeps you from getting to where you want to go. On the other side of the page, turn the negative red light sentence into a positive green light sentence that gets you going on the road toward your goals. A red light sentence such as *I don't have a lot of friends* can be turned into a green light with *I have one really good friend, and we have fun together.* Try to practice using more green light sentences in your thoughts and words every day.

Treasure Chest

We all have things that we save because they make us feel good and happy about ourselves and the best times of our lives.

These treasures can include things like a birthday card from your grandmother that tells you how special you are, a fun photo of you and your friends, a test you studied super hard for and got an A+ on, or a shell from the beach where you go every summer on vacation. Like we did in the "Bank!" activity from chapter 2, gathering up the positives in one place can be a beautiful way to support your empowerment journey.

Take an empty box (shoeboxes are great for this) and start collecting items that make you feel good. Keep adding items over time as more great things happen in your life. When you feel down, you can pull out your treasure chest and look at all these things that make you feel good. Focusing on the good times and positive aspects of your life will leave less time for the things that hold you back!

Star Power

For this activity, you need one cup of flour, one-half cup of salt, and one-half cup of water. Mix the ingredients all together in a bowl and then roll this salt-dough mixture into a ball. Pinch it, knead it, and roll it around. As you do this, imagine the dough represents you right now. You need to know that you exist as a matrix of pure possibilities just like this dough, or molten wax, or moldable clay. Just as these materials can be shaped into anything, you too can reshape and transform.

Now start thinking about some things you would like to accomplish for yourself. Maybe you want to get a part-time job to start saving for a car you want to buy. Maybe you want to spend more time with your grandmother because you two always laugh and have a great time. Whatever it is, start shaping that dough into a star as you think about accomplishing your goal. You just need to believe that your possibilities are endless, and you can shine brightly like a star! Use a straw or pen cap to make a hole in the dough before you let it dry overnight. Once it's dry, you can paint it and even throw some glue topped with glitter on it. Thread ribbon or string through the hole and hang your creation in a visible spot. Let it remind you that you do have the power and the potential to be a star!

Glad Libs

The language we use every day, both in our thoughts and in our words, has an impact on our lives. Over time, words can actually become real. If you've never heard of Mad Libs, it's a word game that comes from the phrase "ad lib," where one player prompts another for a list of words to substitute for blanks in a story.

Using this idea, it's time to turn some of your words into positive outcomes with our Glad Lib activity below. Keep in mind, *ad lib* comes from the Latin phrase *ad libitum*, which means "as you wish." Complete the following Glad Lib or simply make up your own positive statement. Create a recording to listen to, or say it out loud daily for one month. Then assess your progress, and if it's working, keep going until your thoughts become your reality!

I feel so (adjective) about (verb) (noun). I am easily finding (adjective) (noun).

Examples:

I feel so <u>comfortable</u> about <u>taking tests</u>. I am easily finding <u>better grades</u>.

I feel so <u>good </u>about <u>meeting people</u>. I am easily finding <u>new friends</u>.

Keep your statement somewhere close and repeat it out loud or to yourself every day. Watch what you will accomplish.

Lemons and Possibilities

Try this guided imagery that is commonly used by therapists. Close your eyes and picture a lemon slice. Really imagine it—the color, the smell. Pick it up and imagine the texture of the peel. Now that it's in your hand, visualize yourself taking a bite into that lemon. Suck on it and taste how sour it is.

Now open your eyes. Did you notice the actual taste of the lemon in your mouth just from imagining? What you just experienced is the mind's control over the body. It's not necessary for something to *actually* be happening for your body to believe it is. That's the power of the mind. Your body takes its cues from your brain. Write down what you would like to happen in your life. Each night as you are drifting off to sleep, take time to visualize and believe, as if the things you wrote down have already happened. Have fun with this list of possibilities and continue to add to it over time.

Mantra Making

Think of a phrase that resonates with you, makes you smile, and helps you calm down. You can find some examples by searching online for positive mantras. You can make a sign with your mantra on it and place it next to your bed or somewhere that you look each morning when you wake up. You can also use the calendar on your phone to send a reminder to yourself with the mantra, or set it as the wallpaper on your phone so you see it every time you use it. Each time you see your mantra, reflect on its meaning. Enjoy the happiness, calmness, or positivity you feel each time you see your mantra.

Lucky Charms

You may already have a lucky charm. A lucky charm can be any type of item, such as a coin, a certain pair of socks, a piece of jewelry, or a key chain that you feel brings good things your way. The charm, which can basically be anything, helps you to believe that you are actually lucky when you wear it or hold it. Doug Edert, a star player on the St. Peter's University basketball team, which got all the way to the Elite Eight in the 2022 NCAA championship, considered his signature mustache to be his lucky charm.

The important thing to know about a lucky charm is that

even though it helps you to feel lucky, you are the one who can bring good fortune your way. If you don't have a lucky charm yet, experiment with a few items, and see which one helps you. It can be anything from a special pen that you use to get better grades on tests to the pin your grandmother gave you from her travels. Using your lucky charm as a reminder to keep your thoughts positive will certainly help you on the road to where you want to go!

Stick with Positivity

Perhaps one of your teachers in the past placed a sticker on your work when you were younger. When you got home and held up your paper to your family members, showing them that sticker, you probably felt very happy and quite proud. A sticker is like a visual affirmation, from happy faces to positive words, to symbols of holidays and other fun things! They can be purchased online, at dollar stores, and even at high-end specialty stores. If you have access to any of these places and have a few dollars, get some stickers that make you happy and remind you of positive thoughts.

Place those stickers on things that may challenge or frustrate you, to remind you to stay in your positive thinking. For example, placing a four-leaf clover on your geometry notebook may help you feel lucky when solving those problems. Placing a sticker of a sun with sunglasses in your locker can help you start your school day with good vibes. If you don't have access to stickers, maybe you can make your own by printing out a funny or happy picture and covering it with scotch tape, and sticking it wherever you might need it!

Affirmation: I am now empowering myself, one positive belief at a time.

Keep your dreams alive. Understand to achieve anything requires faith and belief in yourself, vision,

hard work, determination, and dedication. Remember
all things are possible for those who believe.
—Gail Devers

Chapter 4: Trust Your Gut

When something feels off . . . it is.
—Abraham Hicks

Affirmation: I trust my intuition and all is well.

Sarah's Story

Sarah got a call on Saturday afternoon from a friend inviting her to a party that night. She accepted the invitation. As soon as she got off the phone, she had a weird feeling in her belly and could not explain it. Sarah was not sure why she was having this feeling, but she wasn't sure she wanted to go at all. This feeling is something Sarah had heard her mom call the "inner compass." That gut feeling is there to help us make the right choices. Sarah's intuition had spoken loudly to her in the past when she was dating someone who was not very kind to her. She ignored that inner voice that was telling her something was wrong for a long time. She learned from that experience that she should listen to her intuition when it speaks to her.

She certainly did not want to disappoint her friend, but after having a conversation about her feelings with her mom, Sarah called her friend and canceled. Her friend surprisingly agreed and said she had had the same gut feeling. Instead, they decided to skip the party and go to the movies. Sarah found out the following day that the police had been called to the party because there was a lot of inappropriate behavior. Trusting her instincts kept Sarah out of trouble, and she ended up having a great time with her friend anyway.

Why You Should Trust Your Gut

The notion of trusting your gut feelings or intuition is real and is grounded in science. The part of our nervous system that manages our gut has been called the body's "second brain" by some people. With the presence of technology in our modern world, people tend to rely on outside factors to help them make decisions about almost everything. Previously, our ancestors relied heavily upon their gut feelings for decision making and for their actual survival. Today, we do not rely on our intuition as much as our ancestors did. We have become dependent on a variety of external sources, including technology, to assist us with our decision making.

Intuition can be thought of as insight that arises spontaneously without thinking. Your intuition's entire mission is to protect you. Some people hear their intuition loud and clear, although it can also be quiet and subtle for others. We all have an intuition, and with practice we can develop a stronger connection and ability to listen to our gut feeling.

Learning to Trust Your Inner Star

Gut Thermometer

A good practice to help you with trusting your gut is to take your "gut temperature" when you need to make a decision. Imagine that you have a thermometer to take your intuitive (gut) temperature. This gut thermometer rises and falls based on what is right and what is wrong for you. When things aren't right, your gut thermometer goes above 100 degrees, just like when you have a fever. At that point, you don't feel right, and you might have actual physical symptoms that go along with feeling sick or feeling that something is wrong. Your stomach might start to hurt, you might feel short of breath, your heart or mind might start to race, and you might feel like you can't eat anything.

If you feel these types of symptoms, like your gut thermometer is above 100, that is the time to reconsider the choice you are about to make. You can ask yourself questions such as *Do I want to do this?* or *How do I feel about this situation?* Your instincts might be telling you that something is actually not good for you. When your intuition is below 100 degrees, you typically feel physically good and fever free. If you are making a decision and your gut thermometer is well below 100 degrees, your instincts may be telling you that that is actually a good decision for you.

Glitter Globes

To help you calm your mind and begin developing your intuition, it's a good idea to have something to focus on. You can create a fun Glitter Globe by filling a jar with a tight-fitting lid halfway with vegetable oil. Fill the rest of the jar with water. Add a few drops of food coloring of your choice and some glitter. When you have an issue that is troubling you and you are not sure what to do, grab your Glitter Globe and shake it up. As you watch the glitter fall and settle, relax your mind and see if an answer to your problem comes to you. You may have to do this several times before you find your intuition guiding you in the right direction.

Mend the End

Think about a situation where you made a wrong choice and it didn't end well. Maybe you decided to stay out late when you knew it wasn't a good idea and your parents grounded you. Maybe you copied the answers from your friend's homework and your teacher called you out on it. Was there something in your head that told you not to do that? Did you kind of know what was going to happen? That was your gut, your intuition, giving you a heads up. Now, reimagine the situation that occurred and listen to your inner voice telling you what to do. It could be saying, *It's time to go home now* or *You know the answers to the homework—do it yourself*.

Imagine yourself listening to what your intuition told you, and mend the old ending of this story, creating a positive outcome instead. Maybe your parents told you they were so proud of you for coming home on time, or maybe you got a 100 percent on the homework assignment you did yourself. When you have to make a difficult choice in the future, listen for that little voice and imagine the positive ending you would like to see.

Body Scan Fan

Become a fan of learning to understand your body better by performing regular body scans, focusing on your body's feelings from head to toe. Throughout the day, notice if you can locate emotions and feelings in your body. Do you feel uncomfortable? Is your body tense? Do you feel anxiety or negative emotions? Is your heart beating fast? Are you relaxed and feeling happy? Is your body at ease, and are you comfortable? Now consider what your feelings are connected to. Is there something going on that is making you feel happy, nervous, or excited? Performing regular scans on your body to get in touch with your emotions will help you connect to your intuition and better know yourself.

Sunny Sides

Spending time in nature can help you become more in tune with your intuition. Wake up early one morning and sit quietly in a safe place outside or by a window and watch the sun rise. Sitting in the dark as the light slowly begins to shine is a powerful metaphor to help you see things with clarity and move toward good decisions in your life. As you watch the light begin to shine, listen to any messages or thoughts that might come into your mind.

As the sun rises every day, it is important to remember every day is a new beginning and can be different from your yesterday. Let your intuition guide you toward doing what your heart knows is the right thing for you. If you don't have access to a place where you can see the actual sun rise, you can search online for *sunrise at the beach* or *sunrise time lapse* and watch videos.

Write Your Way to Right

If you are looking to find an answer to something, or you are having trouble figuring out what to do, grab a pen and some paper and write down whatever comes to mind about the issue. Try to fill the entire page with all of your thoughts about what you should do, could do, and what the right thing to do is. Let your thoughts hit the paper as you begin to explore the options. See if you are led in a certain direction by your writing. Do your words point the way to clarity about what you should do or contain an answer to your question?

Affirmation: I am listening to my body and my feelings and am guided to a better place.

Always listen to your inner voice.
—Oprah Winfrey

PART TWO:
CULTIVATING
POSITIVE QUALITIES

Chapter 5: Have Courage

He who has overcome his fears will truly be free.
—Aristotle

Affirmation: This fear that I am feeling will not stop me from accomplishing my goals.

Mei's Story

Mei had dreaded this day since she took a trip over to the high school from middle school and saw the big monster in the fields behind the school. The rock wall. At that point, she had looked at it and said to herself, *There's no way I'll ever be in the class that has to take on that challenge.* Perhaps she would be out sick that day. Or maybe she would get a note from her mother that said she did not have to participate.

Now, as she stood below it, looking up, she wanted to turn and run the other way. It was so high, and the fall from the top was so far down. The rock climbing wall was fear itself. The night before, she had begged and pleaded with her mother not to send her to school. She was terrified by the thought of having to climb this thing. Yet there was no note from her mother or staying home sick. Her mother said, "Mei, just do what they tell you. Just do it." No sympathy there, for sure.

Mr. Shields, her teacher, came over to check her safety harness. He said, "Mei, now I know you can do this. The trick is don't look down, and take it one rock at a time. You are not expected to get to the top. Just have fun and do your best." Have fun and do your best, he said? *OMG,* Mei thought, *I'm not going to make it. I'm going to fall. People are going to laugh at me.*

"Come on, Mei! You can do it!" said Mr. Shields. Mei grabbed a hold of the rock in front of her and pulled herself up, putting her foot on a rock below. She looked up and saw another rock she could reach, grabbed it, and put her foot on the next rock. She heard someone behind her shout, "Go, Mei!" Wasn't that TJ Porter, one of the most admired students in her class? So, she kept going. One by one, Mei grabbed a rock, pulled herself up, and found another to place her foot on. She heard kids on the ground clapping and cheering. Before she knew it, Mei was at the top of the rock wall! She had made it up to the top, just as Mr. Shields said, one rock at a time.

Why You Should Have Courage

Courage is having the power to face your fears. The choice to be courageous is within your control. We have all had situations in our lives when we were afraid and struggled with having courage. As Yoda says in *Star Wars*, "Fear is the path to the dark side. Fear leads to anger. Anger leads to hate. Hate leads to suffering." When it is difficult to demonstrate courage, we can be held back from accomplishing our goals and making the change we wish to see.

Fear is a natural emotion that can be helpful in some situations by keeping us safe and brave, producing cortisol and adrenaline in our bodies, which help us in those moments. Being afraid is an unpleasant feeling triggered by the perception of danger that is real or imagined, although the results can be the same. If you are fearful and you continue to hold onto that fear, over time your body may suffer, as fear can cause physical symptoms and even illness. If you are worried all the time, your chronic fear can impact many parts of your life. When you lack courage and you need to make clear decisions, you may procrastinate, and this can lead to anxiety or disorganized thinking.

When you are courageous, you demonstrate control and responsibility by taking the first steps. Courage helps you to take risks and do things you felt could be embarrassing in front of your peers. Fear can be exciting for some people, who enjoy things like roller coasters, but these kinds of activities are not for everyone. Those same people may be fearful of something others are not afraid of, like spiders.

When demonstrating courage, it is important to seek help as needed as you begin to take smaller steps out of your comfort zone. Taking small risks is an important part of growing. Still, when working on developing courage, it is important that the risks you take are not putting you in any danger. Asking yourself if the fear that you are concerned about is real or in your mind is an important step in developing courage. When your perceived or real fears become unmanageable, you can always talk to a friend or seek help from a parent, guardian, or counselor.

Ways to Build Your Courage

Rock Star

Take a blank piece of paper and write your goal for one fear you want to conquer. It could be something like applying to a challenging college that you think is out of your league or learning to swim when you are afraid of the water. Starting from the bottom of the page, draw a rock—like one on a rock wall. Inside the rock, write the first step you would need to accomplish to get to your goal. Continue to draw a series of rocks going from the bottom to the top and writing in the steps you must complete to achieve your goal.

If you are not exactly sure what you'll need to do to accomplish your goal, it's a good idea to talk to someone you can trust, like a parent or guidance counselor, to make sure you're not forgetting any of the steps toward reaching your goal. Keep your paper somewhere you can look at it regularly, and start actually taking steps toward your goal. You can color in the rock with a shading pencil or crayon when you have completed a step to keep track of your progress toward your goal.

Place of Peace

When your scary thoughts start getting the best of you, traveling to a place of peace and quiet is a good strategy to find your calm again. You can get there by driving to the beach or walking to the park and hiking up a mountain trail. You may also find your place of peace in your room under your cozy comforter or out in your backyard, sitting on your favorite lawn chair. Use the internet to find earthcams. These will take you to live camera feeds of beaches, resorts, and relaxing areas all over the world. Check out the Windjammer Beach Cam in Lauderdale-by-the-Sea, Florida, and watch a calming sunrise over the ocean, or take a trip to Flying Skunk Farm in West Tisbury, MA, and watch some chickens walking around. Set off to a destination to find your inner Zen and take your mind off your worries.

Furry Friends

One of the easiest ways to release your fears is to spend time with a furry friend, if you enjoy animals and don't struggle with allergies. If this activity is for you, go and pet a dog, cuddle a cat, or feed a fish. Any of these options helps to give you a dose of instant calm and can reduce your fears and negative thoughts. As you enjoy time with your furry friend, imagine the fear releasing into the air around you and traveling far away from you and your pet. If you don't have access to a family pet, you can offer to spend time with a neighbor's pet, volunteer at a local pet shelter, or travel to a store that sells pet supplies and may have shelter animals waiting to be adopted.

Post Your Success

Think about what success looks like in conquering your fear. It could be successfully delivering a speech to the class or climbing the rock wall to the top. Now, on a series of Post-its, write down each baby step you will need to do to get to the place where you conquer your fear. If it's giving a speech to the class, you could start with recording or videoing yourself, and on your Post-it you would write, *I successfully recorded myself giving my speech. I practiced my speech in front of a mirror. I practiced my speech in front of a friend,* and finally *I got up in front of the class and delivered my speech.* When you accomplish each task, put your Post-it up somewhere so that you can see it, and enjoy your success. You've made another move toward accomplishing your goal!

Feel the Fear

Author Dr. Susan Jeffers wrote a book entitled *Feel the Fear and Do It Anyway.* If you enjoy reading, it's a book that you can learn a great deal from with regard to understanding and conquering your fears. If reading is not your thing, go ahead and search YouTube for the book's title and watch a few videos about this. You can use the phrase "Feel the fear and do it anyway" anytime you are working on something you want to conquer. Obviously, please keep it safe and don't do anything dangerous, but let this phrase help get you where you need to be. For example, if elevators make you nervous, the next time you must step into one, say to yourself, *Feel the fear and do it anyway.* You may feel a little bit stronger each time you use these words.

Courage Badge

In the movie *The Wizard of Oz*, the Cowardly Lion struggles with courage throughout the story. In the end, the Wizard gives him a medal badge with the word *Courage* on it. This badge serves to give the lion a sense of strength, and he later sings a song about his confidence. The badge actually helps the lion feel stronger. Choose a piece of jewelry, a patch, a coin, or another valuable item you can wear or carry that will help you feel stronger. This physical item can represent a thought or affirmation that helps you feel courageous and empowered.

Zone Out

Usually when you hear the words *zone out*, you think of someone not paying attention. In this case, we invite you to zone out on fear and begin to make small changes that take you out of your comfort zone. So zone out and go try something new and exciting you have never done before. Pick up a paintbrush and try making some art, to see if you enjoy it. Join a pickup basketball game on the courts and try playing with some new friends. Go to the bowling alley and find out if it is something you enjoy. Zone out on fear by learning something new. Consider going even further by creating a peer group or empower trip group, where you work together trying new activities and experiences. Just be sure to keep it all safe!

Affirmation: I am overcoming my fear as courage is my ally.

The cave you fear to enter holds the treasure you seek.
--Joseph Campbell

Chapter 6: Let It Go

*Time doesn't heal emotional pain, you
need to learn how to let go.*
—Roy T. Bennett, *The Light in the Heart*

Affirmation: When I let go of what I don't need, I know that all of my dreams will come true.

John's Story

When John was ten years old, a neighborhood bully jumped him, pinned him to the ground, and beat him up. When it was over, John didn't realize that his father was watching. Growing up, John's dad was very hard on him. John had no idea what would happen next after his dad witnessed this encounter. His dad certainly had the opportunity to break up the fight and send the other boy on his way, but he did not. When John arrived home, his father was very angry. He proceeded to physically hurt John, and told him never to lose again.

John's dad thought this type of tough love was a way to set high expectations. This message stayed with John for the rest of his life. His dad was not capable of giving John what he needed, like a hug or some words of wisdom. John's dad had also been a victim of abuse, and abuse became his way of parenting. The abuse filled John with anger, and he went after the boy who inflicted the beating on him. This history of abuse caused a great deal of emotional pressure on John, creating a strong drive for him to win and succeed at everything he did. He also struggled with things like asking for help and felt he needed to appear strong. Although John had a lot of friends who were always there for him, he was constantly trying to be independent all the time. It was sometimes a lonely and difficult place to be. Years later John was diagnosed with cancer. John intuitively knew that his need to be tough all the time and his lack of vulnerability contributed to his illness. He learned to embrace change and worked hard on releasing his suppressed emotions. He became more vulnerable and opened up to love, healing, and support. He is currently in remission from his cancer.

Why You Should Let Things Go

When we hold onto negative emotions about a person or a situation, it creates stress inside of our bodies. Anger and chronic stress are linked to six leading causes of death, including heart disease, cancer, lung ailments, accidents, cirrhosis of the liver, and suicide, according to the American Psychological Association. Emotions have the power to weaken your immune system and manifest illness, from an upset stomach to a migraine or even heart disease. Our bodies give us warning signs when we need to shift into self-care. Our bodies talk to us, but we don't always listen.

Letting things go and moving on is a part of everyone's healing journey. Our scars from upsetting events that happened in the past don't go away overnight, but the simple act of letting go and practicing letting go over time is what helps the healing begin. An emotionally traumatic event like the one John experienced can have a lasting impact on a person's life. Stored trauma in the form of anger and aggression from this type of event can be unhealthy. For John, anger was an emotion that was toxic, not only for him but for the others he encountered. In *Men Are from Mars, Women Are from Venus*, John Gray states, "When negative feelings are suppressed, positive feelings become suppressed as well." Anger is a powerful emotion and can be very destructive. At times, anger can also be constructive when it's used to motivate us to work harder in school or at a job, or to win a game.

The most important factor to pursue when you experience anger or any other negative emotion is to understand that you can talk about it. Sharing your emotions with others and expressing your feelings is critical to ensuring that they manifest in a positive way. Anger is a common emotion, and it's very difficult to avoid anger all the time. It is important to release your anger in healthy ways and not hold on to it for too long. There are positive ways to express anger and other challenging emotions that will allow them to disperse and not impact your body, your heart, or other people in a negative way. Talking with someone about these negative emotions can help you to get to the root of what is causing them and will help you to learn to express yourself in a healthy manner.

Abuse like the kind that John experienced will often require the assistance of a professional to begin to recover from. This is not something that most people overcome on their own; if you have experienced abusive behaviors or you struggle with feelings of vengeance, please seek support from safe, trusted adults in addition to working with the helpful self-care strategies laid out in this book.

Learning How to Let Things Go

Shred It

Sit down and identify something someone did to you that upset you that you need to let go of. Write that person a letter about the pain that they caused you and how what they did affected you. This letter should not be shared with the person or with anyone else; it is for your eyes only. Let your pain out in the words of the letter, writing down every detail and allowing yourself to be heard and listened to. End by describing the actions you can take to release this person and their impact on you. Once the letter is complete, and you are ready to let the situation go, begin tearing the letter into small shreds. With each shred that you tear, let your thoughts and anger toward this person float away into the air. With each tear and shred of the paper, you are slowly releasing your negative thoughts about the situation. Once the letter is completely shredded, allow yourself to feel uplifted.

Time Limit

Some people can let things go easier than others. Sometimes an event happens, and even though it's over, we still think about it. The feeling lingers. Giving yourself a time limit for letting things go can be helpful. If you feel comfortable with limiting the amount of time you allow yourself to think about something, then this activity is for you. For example, you can say, *I'll let myself be upset about this until 3:00 p.m., but then I'm done and I will stop thinking about this. I will let this go. I will shift my thinking to something that serves me better.* Declaring something aloud or writing it down when you make a decision can help you.

Spoof Songs

A spoof song is a specific form of parody that involves taking an existing song, keeping the beat and melody the same, then rewriting the lyrics. Creating a spoof song can be a fun way to release anger and other negative emotions by using humor. Spoof songs should not be created to hurt others, and they should not be shared with people as a way of making fun of others or teasing. They should be kept private, but they can offer an opportunity to release what you need.

If you have a class that gets you upset because you don't understand the material, an example would be to take Justin Timberlake's song "I Can't Stop This Feeling" and do a spoof, changing the words to express your feelings, like "I can't stop this feeling. I get mad, mad, mad. All these terms I should know. I feel bad, bad, bad." During this activity, you are using humor to express how mad or bad you feel. It is okay to acknowledge these emotions, and a spoof song provides you with the chance to express them in a healthy way, rather than expressing them through physical violence or holding in your emotions. You can also turn it into a more positive spoof spin after you have overcome the problem or challenge, like "I can't stop this feeling. I'm so glad, glad, glad. I passed my test, and I'm now not sad, sad,

sad."

EX-ORCIZE Your Anger

Exercise, sports, or weight training can offer a healthy outlet for anger and negative emotions. Work with a coach, physical education teacher, family member, or trainer from a gym. This will offer you the opportunity to channel your negative emotions into physical activity. Imagine a release when you are engaged in the activity. For example, if you are upset about the loss of a relationship and using an elliptical machine, imagine you are climbing your way to a healthier connection with someone new. If you are angry about how you were treated by your sibling and shooting hoops, every time you score, imagine them saying something kinder to you. Boxing or martial arts in a structured setting is also an excellent outlet to assist you with releasing anger or upset you may be feeling.

Campaign for a Cause

Consider joining a group that stands for what you believe in and advocate for your rights. If you have been the victim of bullying, groups like StompOutBullying have opportunities for participating in campaigns, serving as peer mentors, and being part of positive social media groups. If you have a family member struggling with addiction, the National Association for Children of Addiction (NACoA) has information and resources just for teens.

You can join a support group, help raise funds, or participate in creative and artistic contests to support causes that are meaningful to you. Simply do your research and speak with an adult you trust to verify that the group you are going to be involved with is legitimate and your safety is a top priority. You can also consider starting your own group if one is not available, so working with your school's social worker or guidance counselor is a good place to begin. Starting small, even with a friend or two, can be powerful in helping you address your concerns.

Mood Grooves

Dancing is an excellent way to release your negative emotions and get some relief from heavy thoughts. You can pick a song that represents what you are going through and move to the beat. You can use your body to express your feelings, stomp and jump, and let all your anger or sadness out in the dance moves. You can do this in private or you can dance with others if you feel comfortable. You also might like to arrange your playlist to play some music that allows you to release your negative emotions first and then move on to some happy and positive tunes when you are feeling better.

Pillow Thoughts

Sometimes not being able to let things go prevents us from sleeping or getting good rest and relaxation. When you retire to bed, you may find yourself overthinking a situation that upset you. You may be replaying an unkind comment someone wrote on Instagram or be upset with a parent for yelling. Sometimes there are fewer distractions when we try to go to sleep at night, so sometimes that's when our thoughts can be at their loudest.

One practice to help you quiet that voice at night is to focus on things that happened in your day that made you feel good, happy, or calm. Your focus does not have to be on big things. Next time your head hits the pillow, think about five positive things that happened in your day. You can choose to focus on small moments, like when a friend smiled at you in the hall, when the teacher acknowledged something you did, or when your mom made your favorite dinner. Try this practice for a week as you drift off to sleep. You can also write positive things that you want to happen and place them under your pillow. Let these thoughts be the last thing you think about before you fall asleep. These thoughts will fill your mind with positivity, help you sleep better, and allow you to wake up to a fresh start the next day with a healthier perspective.

Let It Go!

Letting go, releasing what is bothering you, can free you from what is holding you back. Grab a bunch of pieces of paper. On each one, write down whatever it is that is bothering you. You can simply write down words like *anger* or *hate*, or other things that are bothering you like *failing a test* or *fighting with my parents.* If you love to write, you can even write down an entire story or situation. Once you are done, play the song "Let It Go" from the movie *Frozen*. While you play the song, crumple up the piece of paper and throw it in the trash. Imagine the things or problems that have been bothering you have disappeared and no longer have power or influence in your life. Feel free to sing along with the song at the top of your lungs!

Mean Clean

Find something in your house that really needs to be cleaned. It can be a window, bathroom tub or wall, or a cabinet door. Gather any cleaning products, scrub brushes, or paper towels that are available in your home. Check with your parents that the products you are using are safe. Imagine that the dirt and grime is the negative thought or thing you want to get rid of that is bothering you. Now use your elbow grease and scrub away that dirt and grime, that negative thing in your life!

As you clean, watch whatever you're cleaning begin to sparkle. With each wipe or brushstroke, you are scrubbing out that issue that's bothering you. Once you have removed all the dirt and grime, take a moment to appreciate that you have the power to remove anything negative in your life. Next time something is bothering you, give it a *Mean Clean*!

Open Doors

Think about the expression "When one door closes, another one opens" and apply it to the concept of letting go. When you close the door on one thing, you are opening the door to allow something else into your life. Grab a piece of paper and imagine it's a door. You can even make it look like a door by drawing a doorknob and a knocker or design on it. On the side of the paper with your door, write about what it is you're choosing to let go of. It could be a fear, an unhealthy relationship, a behavior you would like to avoid, or a negative emotion such as anger. Now, as you slowly turn over your paper, imagine it is the door opening to something new for you. Write on this side of the paper what you will allow into your life by closing the door on what you're letting go of. This could include an exciting new hobby, new friends, a healthy lifestyle, or even total happiness. Keep looking for the doors to open in your life as you let go of what no longer serves you.

Nurture Nature

When you let things go, you make room for the new in your life. Consider planting seeds while in the process of letting something go to represent the opportunities for new beginnings. You can do this with some simple potting soil, a container, and herb, microgreen or wildflower seeds. If you are interested, you may even want to investigate small hydroponic gardens for indoor spaces. When you plant your seeds, imagine they're the positive things you're allowing into your life because of what you let go of. As you nurture your seeds and watch them grow, imagine the new in your life flourishing and growing into something much better than the old.

Affirmation: I am relaxed and let go each time I breathe.

The beautiful journey of today can only begin when we learn to let go of yesterday.
—Steve Maraboli

Chapter 7: Be Positive

*If you are positive, you'll see opportunities
instead of obstacles.*
—Widad Akrawi

Affirmation: I see positive changes in my life when I am positive.

Sam's Story

Sam loved math just like her mom and was going to college to study finance. When a neighbor offered her a summer internship at the accounting firm where she worked, Sam jumped at the chance. She worked closely with a woman named Bree, who was the firm's most experienced employee. She learned a lot from Bree and got to know her on a more personal level as well. One day Bree received a call from her brother, who said there was a good chance he could get tickets to a big concert that evening. Bree was so excited about this possibility and talked to Sam about it *all* day! Bree and her brother mapped out their tentative plans. Bree couldn't contain her excitement, and she could barely focus on work. Later, her brother called to tell her he could not get the tickets after all. Sam's heart sank for Bree when she heard the news. Sam sadly said, "You must be so disappointed." Bree replied, "I am a little disappointed, but I haven't been this excited about something for a long time. Even though we are not going, it made for a positive, fun day." Sam was pleasantly surprised by Bree's ability to focus on the positive aspect of the situation. Sam realized that even though we may not get what we want sometimes, we can put things into perspective and still be happy. Bree did not let herself feel disappointed for long and didn't let it ruin her day.

Why You Should Be Positive

Being a positive light in the world and living a positive life filled with kindness and love helps us find happiness. Practicing being more positive can shift your perspective and help you take control of negative thoughts. Anything is possible when we choose to shift our perspective in all aspects of our lives. Research demonstrates that positive and negative thinking influence our brain. Positive thinking contributes to reduced stress and helps to improve mental and emotional health. Negative emotions raise your cortisol levels and can leave you feeling anxious and unstable. When you feel positive emotions, your immune system strengthens. Negative thinking, on the other hand, can bring you down and make you feel depressed. Once you start practicing positivity regularly, you will notice a shift in your mindset. You will feel empowered, and this can lead you to feeling worthy, happy, and confident.

Ways to Be More Positive

See the Light

If you are struggling with something that has happened to you that feels bad or negative in some way, here's a little trick to help you change your thoughts about it. We all experience things that we think are terrible at some point, and later we see that positive things have come out of some of the worst events of our life. Turn off the light in a room and sit in the dark. Whisper or quietly describe the event you feel is horrible. You might say something like "It's terrible that I failed my science test" or "My friend and I had an awful fight" or "My day is ruined because our trip was canceled due to bad weather." Now turn on the light and try to state something positive that can come from what happened. You might say things like "Failing my science test is going to help me study harder on the next one" or "Even though we had a fight, my friend and I are going to be much nicer to each other in the future" or "Our trip is going to be rescheduled, and we are going to have more fun because the weather will be better." It's important to look at the bright side of things, because there really is usually some sort of upside to everything that happens.

Become an Anti-Critic

The poet Maya Angelou once said, "People will forget what you said, people will forget what you did, but people won't forget how you made them feel." It's human nature to want to criticize or judge someone, and it's often very easy to say something negative when you are upset or annoyed with them. If someone isn't doing something harmful or dangerous to you, try working to avoid criticism of that person. Instead, note what is positive about them. A simple way to do this is to use the sentence starter "I like the way you . . ." instead of complaining or critiquing. Instead of saying, "Gosh, you take way too long to get ready," try something like "I like the way you take extra time to get ready because you always look really nice when we go out." Substitute criticisms like "You're really bossy" with something like "I like when you try to give me your best advice. I know you have my best interests at heart." Reframing someone's traits as positive will help you understand their perspective better.

Compliment Karma

The word *karma* is associated with the idea that what you do brings results back to you. There's a cause-and-effect aspect to karma. The idea is that if you do good things, good things will come back to you. Compliment Karma is especially useful for those of us who may feel like no one notices the good things we do or compliments us. To play Compliment Karma, roll a dice or a pair of dice in the morning. (If you don't have dice, you can search the internet for *dice roller* to do this using your phone or computer.) Whatever number you receive on the dice, try giving that number of compliments to other people that day. It's quite likely you will be receiving more compliments yourself since you have started giving so many! That's *Compliment Karma*—you have to give to receive!

Vibrant Visions

If there is something you want to accomplish, improve, or aspire to but you don't have confidence that you can do it, try using this practice of *Vibrant Visions* to help you get there. Determine what it is you are going to focus on. Perhaps you want to score a goal for your team on the soccer field, or have a really good interview and get the job at the local market, or even just have some time for yourself at the beach to relax.

Close your eyes and imagine a vision of yourself doing exactly what you are looking to do. Picture dribbling down the field with no one on your heels, kicking toward the goal, and then jumping for joy after scoring. See yourself confident and answering the questions at the interview with a smile on your face, and then shaking hands with your new boss when they offer you the job. Imagine yourself lying on the beach in the sun, enjoying the rays as the ocean rolls in gently in front of you. You can do this repeatedly over the course of several days to keep your focus on your success. You can keep a journal and write down your vibrant visions as if they were already done. Keeping your visions vibrant will help you to get where you want to go!

Five Positive Things

It's one simple exercise: write down five positive things that happened in your day before you go to bed. Having a positive outlook on your life is the most powerful asset you'll ever have. Positive thinking produces positive emotions inside of you that strengthen your immune system and keep you healthy. It also helps you cope with stress better and feel less depressed and happier! We have this natural tendency to focus on what goes wrong in our daily lives, and we think about it over and over in our heads. We're so quick to notice even the smallest of problems, and we rarely spend any time at all dwelling on the good things that brought us a quick smile or felt good.

Write down five good things that happened in the last twenty-four hours, such as *I had a delicious smoothie, I talked to my friend Suzi, or My sister hugged me.* If you are doing this with someone else, share your positive notes with each other and celebrate how many positive things happened to you both today! This tool is especially good to use during those times when it's so easy to focus on all the stressful, negative things happening.

Sensational Affirmations

Positive affirmations are beneficial words and statements that can help you start to believe the good. If said repeatedly, affirmations start to become reality. Create your own sensational affirmations to experience positive emotions. Use the present tense as if it is already happening. For example, say, *I am learning all the material for my upcoming test* instead of saying *I hope to learn all the material for my upcoming test.*

Always keep your affirmations simple and optimistic. Believe what you write and feel the emotion. The more you say your positive affirmations, the more likely you will be to believe them. Write your affirmations about yourself and say them as often as you wish. Avoid negative words in affirmations such as *no, never, not, don't, can't, won't,* and *will not.* Make your affirmations believable. If you don't feel that something is appropriate for you, such as *My body feels strong and healthy,* you can reframe your affirmation to something you connect with, such as *I am learning to treat my body with respect, and my habits are healthier.* Be patient. Using affirmations may take some time to get your desired results.

Volunteers Deserve Cheers

Spending time offering your services to the community can help to keep you busy so your mind doesn't spend time thinking about negative things. Volunteering for those in need can also help you to realize the fortunate aspects of your life. There are many things to be grateful for!

Ask your guidance counselor about organizations in your community that may be good places for you to volunteer. Local animal shelters, religious institutions, food banks, hospitals, and long-term care facilities are often looking for volunteers. You can also work with your teachers and parents to find a good match for you. Once you start your volunteer service, make sure you cheer yourself on. You are great!

What If?

Are your *What if* thoughts negative? Do you find that they sound like this: *What if I don't get the job? What if I don't pass my exam? What if he doesn't ask me out? What if this? What if that?* We sometimes try to avoid feeling pain and disappointment by expecting the worst. If we put more positive *What if* thoughts out into the world, we will see more positive things happen in our lives.

Challenge your thoughts and flip those negative *What ifs* into positives, so they sound more like this: *What if I get a 100 on my exam? What if I save enough money to get that shirt I want? What if my mom lets me go to the concert?* Pay attention to your thoughts closely to catch your negative thinking. When you practice this, you will naturally catch yourself thinking negative thoughts and feel more and more inclined to flip those thoughts into positives.

Affirmation: I am feeling confident when I think positively.

My dear friend, clear your mind of can't.
—Samuel Johnson

Chapter 8: It's Okay to Play

We don't stop playing because we grow old.
We grow old because we stop playing.
—George Bernard Shaw

Affirmation: I incorporate play into every day.

Kayla's Story

As Kayla sat at her desk in her ninth-period US history class, she couldn't hear a word the teacher was saying. All she heard was *blah, blah, blah*. All she could think about was what she had to do when she stood up from her desk. She had to get to her locker and not forget all the books she needed for homework, go to the Yearbook Committee meeting, then run to catch the late bus, arrive home, and walk Missy the dog, who would no doubt drag her down the street and almost pull her arm out of the socket. Then she would make some mac and cheese for herself and her little brother, clean up the mess, do three hours of homework, look at college websites, and start her college essays.

There was always something! Would she even have time for a few texts with friends tonight? Maybe she would get to sleep by twelve and then tomorrow get up for 7:00 a.m. band practice and do it all over again. It was too much. It was overwhelming, and it was just not fun. At home that night, she could hear the garage door opening; her mom was finally getting back from work. She looked at the clock. It was 9:00 p.m. Her mother worked so hard. How could she tell her mother it was all too much? How could she complain?

She felt like she was about to explode. Kayla needed to relieve some of the stress and pressure she was feeling, because she had no time to simply have some fun. Then she remembered that her mother had told her that she should always talk to her when things were bothering her. As a first step, she decided to talk to her mom. Her mom helped her to come up with a schedule that allowed her to add some things into her week that were fun and enjoyable. Kayla's mom arranged for her brother to go to the afterschool program, allowing Kayla to have some time to do activities she enjoyed. She also hired a neighbor to walk the dog a few times per week. These small changes and some fun extracurricular activities made a significant difference for her.

Why Play Is Important

It's important to find ways to play and enjoy life. According to the National Institute of Mental Health, "Over time, continued strain on your body from stress may contribute to serious health problems, such as heart disease, high blood pressure, diabetes, and other illnesses, including mental disorders such as depression or anxiety." When you do not engage in enough play and enjoyment, the chronic stress will cause your body to respond by producing cortisol.

Play is a remedy for stress, so take some time in your day to have fun. Incorporating fun into your daily routine can help you avoid the negative effects of cortisol, such as weight gain, lack of motivation, and turning to drugs and alcohol. If pressures or responsibilities are making you uncomfortable, nervous, or angry, or having any negative impact on you, you may need to incorporate more play as a strategy to deal with these feelings. Kayla was fortunate because she had a parent who was supportive and willing to listen and help her add fun things into her life. We encourage you to speak with someone in your life who can help you when you need assistance with infusing more play into your routine. Counselors and teachers can assist you if you want help in becoming more playful in your life.

Have More Fun

Play Days

Make sure that you have several days during the week that offer you the opportunity to play and have fun. Incorporate safe things into your week that you truly enjoy. Perhaps you have always enjoyed going to the park and swinging on the swings, playing board games with family members, or playing wiffle ball with your neighbors. Picking up your hairbrush and singing and dancing like you are a Grammy winner can also help to take your mind off stress. Do what feels right for you and have fun. Playing like a kid and jumping on a seesaw or sliding down the slide can bring back positive memories of your childhood and break up the daily grind. Think about what you did for fun when you were younger, and do those enjoyable things again. Have fun!

Kind Time

We all need to schedule Kind Time, time to do something for ourselves, into each day. Even if your schedule is super busy, ten minutes a day of Kind Time can make a positive difference in your life. The easiest way to schedule Kind Time is to think about a time during the day when you will most likely be free and set the alarm on your phone for Kind Time. During that time, you should do something you enjoy. You can listen to music, spend time with friends, take a walk, play with a pet, play a video game, take a bubble bath, or whatever makes you happy. It's important to schedule it so you don't forget to take care of yourself and do something that helps you de-stress each day!

Mind Rewind

Push the rewind button on your mind and think back to a time when you were super happy. What were you doing? Who were you with? What was it about that time that made you feel so good? Maybe you were in your grandmother's kitchen and she was cooking up your favorite dish. You may even be able to still smell it! Maybe you were in your backyard, running around laughing your head off with your rambunctious dog. Take a moment to feel the happiness. Sit back and enjoy the smile that Mind Rewind just gave you. Now think about how you can create some special moments that make you happy in the present. It may be very different from what made you happy in the past.

Magic Carpet

Take a towel or a blanket and spread it out on the floor. Sit in the middle of it and grab the two front corners. Close your eyes. Now imagine you are lifting off the floor and your magic carpet is taking you to your absolute favorite place. Land your carpet at your chosen place and create your experience. It could be the beach, it could be the basketball courts, or it could even be Paris in front of the Eiffel Tower. What do you see? Waves? Friends shooting hoops? A beautiful city? What do you feel and smell? The breeze and salt air? Warm heat from the asphalt court? Perfume the person next to you is wearing? Fly around this beautiful place on your magic carpet and see all the wonderful things it has to offer. After you are done enjoying your time at this special place, you can return home on your blanket to your present moment, but try to stay with the happiness you felt as you traveled on your journey.

Peace Paint

Use this activity on a day when you are super stressed out and really need to calm yourself and forget your troubles. All you need is a paintbrush. Imagine there is a puddle of pure paint in front of you infused with healing, calming diamond light. Now dip your paint brush in the imaginary paint and use it to paint yourself with peace. Start at your fingertips and paint your hand. Move to your arms and continue to feel the peace wash over you. You can paint peace over your entire body and feel the total relaxation cover you. You can always repaint yourself again if you need it.

You can also keep your imaginary peace paint on for the day to shield you from any negativity that might come your way. Or paint an actual picture of what peace looks like to you using the same paintbrush and watercolors or tempera paints. If you don't have access to paint, draw it with whatever supplies you have.

Comic Relief

When you really need to escape from the things that are troubling you, take some time for comic relief. Watch a comedy series, a funny movie, or your favorite comedian and enjoy some good laughs to change your mood and relax your nerves. We have all heard that laughter is the best medicine, and getting some good giggles can keep your mind in a peaceful place. Laughing alone is a great feel-good tool and is very healing. You can also do this with friends and just do silly things that make you all laugh. Make funny noises, watch silly cat videos, do whatever really cracks you up.

Affirmation: I am playful and live happily.

It's the things we play with and the people who help us play that make a great difference in our lives.
—Fred Rogers

Chapter 9: Stellar Serenity

Serenity is the tranquil balance of heart and mind.
—Harold W. Becker

Affirmation: As I inhale serenity surrounds me, and as I exhale I release all stress and tension.

Ahmad's Story

Ahmad sat slumped in his chair with his math book covering his view of the teacher. *Please don't call on me, please, please, please!* he thought to himself. He could feel his heart beating faster and faster. He could barely see the numbers and lines in front of him. They got blurrier and blurrier. They started to move on the page. He was terrified. It was his worst nightmare. It was fractions. Fractions drove him crazy. They made him nervous. He just could not understand them. When he saw fractions or someone even mentioned them, he actually started to feel like he was going to throw up.

And then it happened. Mrs. Sealey said, "Okay, Ahmad, what decimal is one-half equal to?" He started to breathe heavily. "Ahh," he said, "umm." He couldn't speak. The panic was more than he could bear. "Ahmad," Mrs. Sealey said, "you know this. Use your calculator if you forget." Ahmad could barely pick up his calculator, but he did and just started pressing buttons over and over. Mrs. Sealey looked at him with the kindest eyes. She said, "Oh, I think I know how to explain this better, Ahmad." She went to the whiteboard and wrote the number one-half on the board. Then, next to the number one, she drew what looked like an egg with hands and feet.

Then she drew a parentheses next to the number two and

a vertical line on top of it, creating the long division sign, and said, "Humpty Dumpty sat on a wall, Humpty Dumpty had a great fall." She moved the number one under the long division sign. Ahmad looked at what she had done. *Woah . . . wait*, he thought. *Are fractions division problems?* The panic seemed to leave his body. Once Ahmad relaxed, he realized that his anxiety was keeping him from thinking straight. Now it seems so simple. He picked up his calculator. Was one half simply one divided by two, like Mrs. Sealey had shown him on the board with Humpty Dumpty? He put the number one in his calculator and divided it by two and got the answer .5. He looked at Mrs. Sealey in disbelief. He said, "Is it .5?" Could that be right? "Yes!" Mrs. Sealey shrieked in delight. "What is one-fourth?" she asked. Ahmad put the numbers in his calculator. "It's .25" he said. "Correct!" Mrs. Sealey said. And that was the day Ahmad was no longer scared of fractions anymore, thanks to Humpty Dumpty! They never made him nervous again.

Why Should You Stay Serene

When you stay calm and serene, you can focus better on your ability to make decisions and problem solve. Learning to calm your mind helps you to alleviate stress and anxiety and improves your attention span. A calm mind allows you to sleep well, and when you are rested, you perform better. Staying calm helps you to remain positive and allows you to be more creative. When you are relaxed, you are able to lead a more balanced life, taking advantage of opportunities and recognizing which factors can lead you down the wrong path, to drugs and alcohol, for example. Research indicates that when you are calmer, you can communicate better and avoid fighting. According to studies, mindful relaxation can actually change your emotions, training your nervous system to be resilient. You are able to physically and emotionally lead a healthier life.

Ways to Stay Serene

Need the Dough, Knead the Dough

A simple salt dough can be made at home with two cups of flour, one cup of salt, and one cup of water. This dough will not be edible, so do not eat it. Once you combine the ingredients, use your hands to mix and squeeze them together using your fingers. Place the dough on the counter and start pressing it down with two hands, then roll it into a ball. Pinch it, press it, smack it, pick it up, and drop it! Swat it, poke it, pound it, and roll it into a snake. This process is called kneading the dough, and sometimes when you are really nervous, *needing* to *knead* the dough can really help you forget your worries. There is something very calming and relaxing about putting your hands in a wad of dough and simply pushing it around, rolling it, flattening it, and just having fun. You can also turn this dough into a sculpture, use cookie cutters, paint it, or do whatever you want with this dough (except take a bite) once it dries! Next time you're worried, Need the Dough, Knead the Dough.

Shower Power

Before you get in the shower next time, think about what is sticking to you from your day that you would like to get rid of. Did someone say something unkind to you? Are you worried about how you did on your math test? Are you annoyed because your sister wore your favorite shirt? As you take your shower, imagine the water washing away whatever was bugging you. Watch that problem or worry go right down the drain, and as it goes away, say goodbye and good riddance. Leave the shower feeling refreshed and renewed!

Sound Healing

Do an internet search for *homemade wind chime* or *upcycled wind chime* and start this fun project to feel more serene. You can tie together anything, from old silverware to seashells, to create your own wind chime. Sitting outdoors and listening to the sounds of the chimes can be extremely healing and relaxing. Sound bowls, steel tongue drums, and tuning forks are all things that can be purchased that you may want to experiment with to help you listen to healing, soothing vibes.

Bubble Your Troubles Away

You can purchase bubbles at a local dollar store or grocery store. You can also make your own bubbles using one-half cup of dish detergent, one and a half cups of water, and two teaspoons of sugar. Use the wand that comes with the bubbles, or a straw, and blow the bubbles. For larger worries, you can blow bigger bubbles. Imagine you are releasing your problems as the bubbles float away and burst into the air. Enjoy watching your troubles leave you.

Breathe Easy

Deep breathing is a practice that enables more air to flow into your body and can help calm your nerves, reducing stress and anxiety. One breathing exercise, called "box breathing," is used by Navy SEALS. This practice is simple and effective. Take a deep inhale of air for four seconds and hold it for four seconds. Exhale for four seconds and hold it for four seconds. Do this at least three times or more until you start feeling more relaxed. When using this method, inhale through your nose with your stomach expanding while you inhale. You can actually feel yourself calm down. Do this anywhere, even in class.

Have a Hobby

Having regular hobbies keeps your mind busy, fulfilled, and relaxed. If you aren't sure what hobby is for you, start trying new things and see what you enjoy. Do some research by searching YouTube for alternative forms of exercise such as qigong, tai chi, yoga, etc. Journaling, listening to music, gardening, playing an instrument, and reading are activities that can help take your mind to a positive place. Consider dancing, hiking, or other traditional sports like running, lacrosse, basketball, or even high-intensity interval training (HIIT). You can also show your creativity with activities such as cooking, making art, writing poetry, or even roller-skating. All of these activities are good outlets for stress and may help you to stay serene and relaxed.

Social Media Cleanse

Social media certainly has its benefits, but the downside is that you can feel like you have to keep up with your peers for approval or some kind of rating. You may see friends posting pictures and commenting about things that cause you to feel uncomfortable. You might also see negative comments that can impact the way you feel, leading to anxiety. To support your serenity, it is important to limit your time on social media and spend more time in the real world.

Try a Social Media Cleanse and do not sign into any social media for an entire day. Assess your stress level and think about your feelings after this detox. You can also try doing this for longer, or you can have a challenge with friends or at school to see how long you can avoid signing in. You might also pick a day of the week and have a ritual, like Media-Free Fridays, where you simply stay off all social media.

One Magic Minute

Meditation, no matter how short, has been proven to have numerous benefits on our mental and physical health. Meditation reduces stress, increases attention span, helps improve your sleep, and decreases blood pressure. To start your one magic minute, stop what you are doing and take a deep breath in, feel your body, and breathe out. Make breathing in and out your only responsibility. Listen to your breath as it goes in and out of your nose. Feel it as it fills your lungs. Control it as your lungs empty. What do you feel, hear, or experience? Do this for one minute. You can incorporate this into your day at any time to help increase your relaxation level. You can also add more time to your one magic minute and meditate for longer.

Affirmation: I am learning to be calm and relaxed.

Take a large magnifying glass and go outside in nature and just observe the micro world. It's a great first step to understand your place in the world and to find yourself.
—Sonya Renee Lawrence

PART THREE: FINDING HARMONY WITH OTHERS

Chapter 10: Forgiveness

Remember, we do not have to know how to forgive.
All we have to do is be willing to forgive.
—Louise Hay

Affirmation: When I forgive myself, forgiving others becomes easier.

Anna's Story

Anna lived in a neighborhood where bullying had become common, and she was targeted one summer night in the park by several boys and girls. One girl had it out for her more than the others. Anna did not know why. She wasn't hurt physically but was emotionally attacked and humiliated. She was angry after the event and wanted revenge. She later told her older brothers and sisters, who wanted to back her up. Anna went to the park with her family and confronted the bullies. Anna looked into the girl's eyes, saw her fear, and decided to stop.

Once Anna stopped, the girl and her friends started to apologize. Anna was shocked, because she always considered this group to be pretty tough. The apology helped Anna realize that revenge was not going to make her feel happy. It would only cause more hate and anger. They all went to the same school and would have to see each other in the future every day. Forgiveness was the only action that made sense to Anna at that time. She didn't want to ever cause anyone to feel the pain she felt. Choosing to forgive the bullying left Anna in a place where she felt stronger and more empowered. When Anna saw the girl in the hallways in the future, she was able to say hello and keep moving past what had happened.

Why Forgiveness Is Important

When someone does something wrong to you, you may begin to dislike the person or become extremely angry. If you don't address your feelings, they can become toxic and can cause harm to your body. There is scientific evidence to show that negative thoughts and feelings can actually cause disease. To prevent this, learning to forgive is an effective intervention. Studies show that people who are more forgiving tend to be happier and have less depression, stress, anxiety, anger, and hostility. Forgiveness calms stress levels, which can lead to overall improved health. When learning to forgive, it does not mean that you are dismissing what someone has done to you. It simply means that you are letting go of a feeling that is harmful to you, for your own benefit.

Making a conscious decision to let go of any negative emotions will help you release the feelings of anger and resentment. By releasing anger, you may begin to look at the other person with empathy and understanding. Some situations may initially require additional discussion and assistance from adults to determine if they are situations that are forgivable. Although forgiveness is important, there are some situations, such as those that have left physical or emotional harm, that may require professional help to work through. If an individual who is perpetrating bullying or other unkind acts is unwilling to stop or apologize, forgiveness is unlikely to change the situation. Help may be required from parents, teachers, mental health professionals, or even law enforcement in cases of severe bullying.

Forgiving ourselves is also as important as forgiving others. Looking at our own mistakes, and having compassion with ourselves too, is an essential part of forgiveness. Forgiveness can lead you to more happiness, joy, and peace.

Learning to Forgive

The Art of Forgiveness

There are many symbols that represent forgiveness, like an olive branch, a peace sign, a dove, etc. Do an internet search for symbols representing forgiveness and select one that resonates with you, to remind yourself to forgive when you need to. You can also create your own symbol if you wish. Select a small rock from your garden or backyard and paint your symbol on your rock, using tempera paint, acrylics, paint pens, or even a sharpie. Keep your rock somewhere close to remind yourself of the importance of forgiveness.

Tear Tears

Take a piece of paper and draw a large teardrop on it. Think of someone who has done things to hurt you that you want to forgive. Write down the things this person has done to you. It is normal to feel hurt, anger, or sadness when thinking and writing about these things. Once you have written down all the hurts, begin tearing the paper into shreds while thinking about forgiving the person who did you harm. As you tear, repeat to yourself, *I forgive you.* Let all the anger, hurt, and sadness leave you as you tear the page. Once you have finished tearing up the paper, sit for a moment and feel the power of the forgiveness you have given.

Forgive Me Poem

Search the internet for poems about self-forgiveness, for example, "The Mountain" by Laura Ding-Edwards. Once you have read it, think about what this poem means to you. To be able to forgive others, you first must be able to forgive yourself. Consider an area of your life where you need to forgive yourself. Write your own poem about forgiving yourself, and begin to forgive and love yourself a little every day. You can reread the poem as often as you need until you feel you are forgiven.

Here's an example of a forgiveness poem:
I choose to love
I choose to forgive
This is how I want to live
Life is beautiful

I see the joy all around me
This is how I choose to be.

Send Love to Their Heart

Using visualization can help you practice forgiveness toward someone who has hurt you. Visualization in the simplest terms is making a movie in your head. If you feel you are ready to forgive someone, picture yourself in your mind standing across from the person. Imagine heart emojis traveling in the air from your heart center to theirs. While you are doing this, say to yourself, *I'm sending love to your heart. I'm sending love to your heart. I'm sending love to your heart.* Do this several times.

Forgiveness Interview

Interview your friends or family and ask them about a situation when they chose to forgive someone. What did the person do to them that caused them to be angry or hurt? Ask them to share what strategies they used to forgive the person and how they got over their anger and hurt. Consider how you can use what you learned from this interview to forgive someone in your life.

Forgiveness Meditation

If you are having difficulty forgiving someone, there are many free videos that can help you with this. Do a search on YouTube for *guided forgiveness meditations*. Sample the meditations and see which one resonates with you. There are many resources available to help you on your path to forgiveness, and finding support online is easy. Consider talking with a guidance counselor, adult you trust, or parent to find further support on your path toward forgiveness if needed.

Forgiveness Ad

Imagine you are asked to create a forgiveness campaign that will reach people of all ages in your community. You can get inspiration by researching memes that relate to forgiveness. Once you determine a message for your campaign, create a sign or ad that represents your forgiveness message. Make sure that your ad uses appropriate language and is not offensive. Most grocery stores or libraries have bulletin boards that allow people to post signs. Hang your sign somewhere in the community, or post it on your social media to spread your message of forgiveness.

Forgiveness Self-Talk

Consider a time when you said or did something hurtful to someone else. Ask yourself if your actions were avoidable. What emotions were triggered to cause you to say or do something hurtful to the other person? Was there a better way of handling the situation? How can you handle this type of experience in the future? It is important to forgive your past mistakes and actions because everyone makes mistakes. Say the following to yourself: *I forgive you. I forgive you. I forgive you.* The next time you catch yourself starting to say or do something hurtful to someone, consider what you are feeling and reflect before you act or speak.

Affirmation: I am healing my heart when I forgive others.

Forgiveness is the attribute of the strong.
—Mahatma Gandhi

Chapter 11: See Others' Perspective

When you change the way you look at things,
the things you look at change.
—Wayne Dyer

Affirmation: When I listen to others, I will be open to seeing their perspective.

Sunny's Story

Sunny wanted to go to his friend's house for a bonfire on Friday night. It sounded like so much fun, and he was really looking forward to it. He was told his friend's father would be home to make sure the kids were supervised. Sunny's mom agreed to let him go and planned on meeting the dad in person when she dropped Sunny off. When she arrived, no parents were home. Sunny tried to convince her not to worry. He told her he would be fine alone and begged her to leave him there to enjoy time with his friends. She refused, and they argued for a few minutes. Sunny thought his mom was being unreasonable. He was angry she didn't trust him to stay out of trouble. He argued about what a good kid he was, and he wanted her to give him some space to hang out with his friends. After Sunny realized his mom was not going to leave, he went inside to find his friend, to ask where his dad was. While Sunny was in the house, the father pulled up into the driveway. He told Sunny's mom he'd just run out to pick up a few pizzas for the kids. That was all she wanted, and she felt good about leaving.

When she arrived later to pick Sunny up, he got in the car. He thought about his friend Joey, who always had so much freedom to do what he wanted without any supervision. Sunny was once jealous of Joey's life, but at the party, he noticed Joey engaging in a lot of loud and unruly behavior. As the night went on, Sunny thought about the times Joey had gotten into trouble and wondered, *Can he even control himself?* Sunny started to feel grateful that he had a mom who was looking out for him. He felt lucky she loved him that much. He saw the situation from her perspective and felt bad about giving her such a hard time when she dropped him off. He realized that Joey did not have the same support at home that he did. On the ride home, he promised his mom to try to see her perspective in the future. He also spoke to her about how he could be a person who could be there for Joey in the future.

Why It's Important to See Other's Perspective

Misunderstandings happen easily when we assume that everyone sees things from the same perspective as we do. It can be difficult to see things from someone else's viewpoint. Everyone has a unique perspective because of what they have been through in their own lives. When you take time to learn about where someone is coming from, you are gathering evidence that helps you gain an understanding of their perspective. Taking another's perspective helps us to understand situations from other people's positions, beliefs, values, and experiences. When we are open to seeing things from another's side, we practice less judgment, we tend to have less conflict, and it can lead to us having healthier relationships. According to the American Psychological Association, "psychological perspective-taking is a powerful social cognition that helps us to understand other people. It creates feelings of closeness and sympathy, motivates us to help others, and is important for positive social relationships."

Learning to See Other's Perspective

Listening Pro

Pick a song and listen to the lyrics with a friend. As you listen, consider what the lyrics mean to you. At the same time, have your friend think about what the lyrics mean to them. What messages are you both getting? When the song ends, share with your friend what messages you received and what the song meant to you. Have your friend share the same back with you. Did you both think or feel similar things? What did you each see differently? If you saw things differently, talk with your friend about your own perspectives. After you finish, search the internet for the song to see what the artist's interpretation of it was. Talk with your friend about how it was the same or different from what you each perceived.

One Question

Listening helps you to gain a better understanding of the other person's perspective. When someone is stressed, try asking one question: "How can I support you?" Once you ask this question, simply listen to what the person says. This is a powerful question that you can keep tucked away in your toolbox when a friend or family member comes to you with a problem. Practice asking this question instead of giving advice or making suggestions, and see for yourself how well it is received. Questions lead to evidence, and evidence leads to understanding. Understanding leads to better awareness and appreciation of the other person's perspective.

Role Reversal

If you are having a disagreement with someone, it's sometimes fun to try reversing roles. If you can both agree and the situation is not serious, reversing roles can sometimes help to lighten the mood and make finding a solution easier. Try to pretend you are an actor or actress, and swap places with the person you are having the dispute with. Act the part of the other person and use the words and gestures they use. Actually pretend to be them, and have them pretend to be you.

For example, if you are having a disagreement with your guardian about going to a party and they keep telling you things like "I don't want you drinking" and "What if there's a fight?" play that part and repeat their words and gestures. If your words are "Leave me alone" and "Nothing is going to happen," have your guardian say those words back to you.

After you complete this activity, talk with your guardian about it. Can you see things from their side? What do you think about how this person sees you? Is there anything you would like to change about your behavior? You can also do this with a friend and have fun playing each other's part. If it's a serious situation, it may be a good idea to see a counselor or adult instead, to help resolve the problem or facilitate the role reversal.

Getting the Picture

If you are having a problem meshing with someone and you're not really getting along, try doing a photo swap with the person to get a better understanding of them. Have them share three socially appropriate photos from their cell phone that are meaningful to them and have a story behind them. Ask the person to share their stories with you about the photos. Ask them to explain why these photos are meaningful to them. Pay attention to what they share and make mental notes as you try to really get to know this person. Next, share three socially appropriate photos of yourself and explain the same to them. Talk about the details and why these images are so meaningful to you. After doing this activity, do you see the person differently, since you have taken time to get to know them better? What have you learned about them and about yourself?

Ambiguous Images

If you search the internet for *ambiguous images*, you will find various pictures that can appear to be at least two different things depending upon how you look at them. Consider how this applies to situations in your life. Depending on what perspective you take, and what perspective others may have, the same thing can look quite different to different people. The next time you are in a disagreement or a situation that you don't understand, consider these images and try to find a way to see the situation differently.

Change the Moment

Misunderstandings can happen if we don't ask questions and try to understand the other person's side of things. When you understand the person's feelings and perspective, it can increase your empathy and enable you to have more positive interactions. Ask questions the next time you are on the brink of a disagreement with someone. Don't be afraid to communicate before things escalate. For example, the next time you start to disagree with someone, before arguing back, ask the person, "Why is this so important to you?" By asking this simple question, you will be able to gain an understanding of their perspective and where they are coming from. You will also be able to shift the dynamics of the conversation from anger or annoyance to understanding and clarity.

Affirmation: I am a good listener because I have an open mind.

*Everything that irritates us about others can
lead us to an understanding of ourselves.*
—C. G. Jung

Chapter 12: Understand the Truth

If you do not tell the truth about yourself,
you cannot tell it about other people.
—Virginia Woolf

Affirmation: When I understand the truth, I have peace of mind.

Kyle's Story

Kyle was standing at his locker when his friends approached him and started telling him about Jeffrey being thrown off the basketball team for cursing at the coach. Kyle, who is also on the basketball team, got really upset at this because Jeffrey was one of their star players. The big game was coming up at the end of the week, and if Kyle was no longer on the team, they would not win. Kyle started getting really upset, slammed his locker door, and ended up hurting his finger. Now, with a throbbing finger, Kyle stormed down the hallway toward Jeffrey's locker.

Jeffrey was standing at his locker, and Kyle proceeded to yell at him, asking, "What's wrong with you? Why did you curse at the coach? Now we don't have a chance of winning the game because you got kicked off the team!" Jeffrey had a puzzled look on his face and proceeded to explain to Kyle that he did not curse at the coach. He told Kyle that he missed a shot and said a curse word, and the coach pulled him into his office and reminded him to use appropriate language on the court. Kyle stood there, holding his sore finger, realizing that he should have gotten the facts from the source before he reacted.

Why Understand the Truth

Accurately understanding the truth allows you to make rational decisions with clarity. Finding out if the data you're considering is accurate allows you to weigh your thoughts and form an opinion based on facts. Making a rational decision based on things that are not true can be dangerous and lead to consequences you did not intend. When we see things clearly and don't construct stories in our minds that don't exist, our decisions may be sound and more accurate.

Listening to gossip and passing judgment on others can have negative consequences for us and the other person. When we assign things meaning before we know the truth, we have a flawed understanding of reality. We can sometimes react to what we think is the truth and be completely wrong and off base if we don't have all the facts. Today, we must exercise caution due to the presence of mistruths on social media and television. Accurately documenting historical facts and conducting scientific research are examples of the process of getting to the truth. Observing and recording things accurately and analyzing the results helps us to act in an informed and more responsible manner.

How to Better Understand the Truth

CSI

The next time you hear a rumor that you question, you have two choices. You can stay out of it and avoid spreading the rumor. You can also consider doing your own investigation into the situation if it's about a close friend that you feel you need to inform about the rumor. If you think it's important to tell your friend that there is a rumor about them, talk to the people who are spreading the rumor. Ask them how they know what they are saying is true. Can they provide solid evidence that what they're saying is accurate? Ask them who they heard the rumor from.

Once you feel you have a good understanding of what is being said and who said it, talk to the person who is the subject of the rumor. You can say something like "I just want to give you a heads up that people are saying _____ about you, and I think you should know." Be there for your friend to provide support and listen if they have something to share or need to talk about. Consider encouraging your friend to speak with a teacher, counselor, or parent if the situation is something more serious.

Rewrite

Think about a time when a rumor did harm to you or someone you know, and rewrite the ending to that story. In your mind, think about the situation and the feelings that it caused. Mentally flip the scenario, and imagine any negative actions that others may have taken transforming into positive actions that solved the problem and got to the truth behind the gossip.

For example, perhaps you were accused by your teacher of cheating or copying a homework assignment when you really didn't do that. Maybe someone in the class was jealous of your good grades and decided to report this falsely to the teacher. Reimagine the ending of the story so that instead of the person reporting a lie to the teacher, they actually came to you and told you they were jealous of your grades. Instead of reporting the lie to the teacher, you worked together, studied, and both improved your grades in the end. In the future, when dealing with rumors, try to keep in mind what you can do to create a positive outcome for all the people involved. If you see friends' actions starting to create something negative in the future, you can ask your friends what they can do instead to create a positive outcome.

Fact Checker

Google's Fact Check Explorer allows you to check facts about various people. Enter the names of some of your favorite celebrities. Have you heard some of these stories before? Notice the stories that have been posted on social media about the person, and consider if the information was actually true or false. Did you believe the information you are now finding out is not accurate? Notice how many stories have been posted that contain inaccurate information. Consider how much of the information you are receiving each day is actually accurate. Does this make you rethink the accuracy of the information classmates or friends may be sharing about each other? Think about what you can do in the future to ensure you are getting the most accurate facts.

True or False?

You can do this activity with a friend or a group of friends. Each of you should write down a total of three things in a random order. Two of the things you write down should be things that you think no one would guess about you that are actually true. For example, you might have traveled to the Swiss Alps when you were five, or you may have a collection of two hundred baseball cards. One of the things you write down should be completely made up and untrue but something you think people could possibly believe.

Exchange papers and try to guess which of the things are the true facts about the other person and which thing was made up. When you find out what the actual facts were, talk with your friend or friends about how accurate your guesses were. Was it more difficult to believe the things that were actually true, or did you believe the false fact? Talk about what you learned by doing this activity and consider how it can relate to dealing with gossip and rumors in the future.

Lateral Reading

Lateral reading is a way to fact-check and verify the accuracy of a source to make sure you are getting the most accurate information online. Instead of staying on one page to deeply research a topic to get information, you would open multiple pages and skim the information to look for consistency, author bias, and other things that can skew the information you are receiving. In lateral reading, you look for consistent messages about something from multiple sources and avoid only using one source when you need to learn more. The next time you are researching a topic for a paper or project, try using lateral reading to make sure you're getting accurate and unbiased information. You can use YouTube to watch videos and develop your skills related to lateral reading. You can include Stanford University in your search as they have extensive videos on this topic to help you learn more. For additional support, consider asking for instruction on lateral reading from your English teacher.

Unicorns

Unicorns are real. When you read this sentence, it is quite likely that you don't agree with the accuracy of the statement. Now use your search engine to ask, *Are unicorns real?* Click on and skim through at least fifteen of the resources that show up. Does your opinion change about the existence of unicorns, and if so, how? How did the research, particularly as it relates to science, influence your opinion after your investigation? How important is research in finding out the truth? Share this activity with a friend, family member, or teacher and see what interesting conversations this can spark. You can also consider researching other topics of interest and use the steps above.

Affirmation: I am clear in my thinking and understand the truth.

All truths are easy to understand once they are discovered. The point is to discover them.
—Galileo Galilei

Chapter 13: Look for the Good in Others

When you choose to see the good in others,
you end up finding good in yourself.
—Various

Affirmation: I love all the good people in my life and will continue to love all the others I will meet.

Stacey's Story

Growing up, Stacey's home life felt unstable and sometimes scary as she watched her parents fight pretty often. Her dad drank too much, and her mom would scream, cry, and even throw dishes at him. Her dad would sometimes put their family in jeopardy, driving while drinking and spending money they needed for food. Stacey spent a lot of time at her uncle's house while her mom worked nights as a waitress because her dad wasn't well enough to take care of them. This instability in her home led her to develop an excessive need to control other aspects of life.

We naturally develop our own strategies to survive, and Stacey's was to control whatever she could. This helped her feel safe in an unsafe environment. Stacey experienced deep feelings of shame throughout her life, well into her adulthood. When she reached her midthirties, she recognized the resentment and anger she'd felt toward her dad for all those years. This shame had triggered her throughout her life, and she blamed her dad for this issue. She knew her feelings were valid and that it wasn't her fault she had a traumatic childhood. Still, she felt very aware of this blame and anger and its negative impact on her.

So she began to work on looking for the good in her father, in an effort to have a healthier relationship with him. She practiced shifting her focus away from his past behavior. She chose to focus on the good in him in the present moment. She was surprised how easily she found so much good. She had no idea that she had been holding on to that much of his wrongdoing in her heart. Her dad was a loving and giving person. Making this decision allowed them to grow closer. She was able to see him through a new lens. They are both standing in a very different place today. She now gets to enjoy his love because she made that choice.

This story deals with the particularly adverse experience of addiction in a parent. It is important to note that Stacey made this decision about her father when she became an adult with her own agency over her life. It is not a child's fault if they are adversely affected by a parent's behavior, nor is it a child's responsibility to fix a parent. Likewise, it is not a young person's job to repair a relationship with a parent who is having addiction issues. If you find yourself in a similar situation, you may wish to seek support from a school social worker, guidance counselor, or other safe and trusted adult.

Why Look for the Good in Others

Everyone you'll ever meet will have at least a few positive attributes. Believe it or not, even bullies do have some good qualities. Some experts say that when we look at others, we actually recognize or identify with something in that person that exists in ourselves. Just as you can look into a mirror and see your flaws, you can look at someone else and see theirs too. Humans can tend to look at people's bad qualities over their good ones because pointing out others' shortcomings can help them feel better about themselves.

Looking for the good in others instead of focusing on the negative has many benefits. This practice is just like eating healthy or working out. If you are consistent, it can help you develop positive emotions. Studies show that positive emotions can strengthen your immune system, make you healthier, and increase your self-esteem. Practicing seeing the good on a daily basis can help your relationships grow stronger and healthier. It can positively improve the way you work with others, and it benefits you and everyone around you. When we focus on the beauty in people, we have the potential to experience more peace and happiness.

How to Look for the Good in Others

Selfie Work

Use your phone to view yourself on the camera as if you are taking a selfie. Look at yourself on the screen and say something good to yourself. Take the time to give yourself a few compliments. Stick with things that go beyond the physical characteristics like *Your hair is great* or *Your makeup is perfect*. You can say things such as, *I am responsible,* or *I take really good care of my sister*. You can do this several times over the course of a week and see how you feel. Now that you have been able to say positive things about yourself, think of someone in your life you like. Record a short video where you compliment that person for their good qualities and send it to them. Notice how they react and how it makes you feel when you offer compliments to others.

Refocus Your Lens

Think of a character from a movie who has memorable negative qualities. These could include bullying, using mean words, or engaging in harmful acts. It's so easy to focus your lens or view on someone's negative qualities. If you dig deep, you'll find some good ones too. For example, think of Cruella de Vil from the movie *101 Dalmatians.* Some of her negative qualities include violent mood swings, having a nasty temper, being self-centered, and acting spoiled. If you had to pick a few good qualities, you could say she was also confident, smart, strategic, and independent. Now, think of a different character from a book or movie with negative characteristics. Identify three negative qualities of this character. As you look for the good and refocus your lens, what are three positive things about this person? Are they smart, strong, ambitious, patient, responsible, or confident? You can also do this activity with a friend. There is good in everyone, and most people can be filtered through an optimistic lens. You can also select someone in your life and apply this activity to them, refocusing your lens and looking for the good.

Positive Posts

Post five positive comments on friends' timelines each day. Try to look for people who are not receiving a lot of likes or comments when you do this. When you are commenting, try to avoid superficial or materialistic comments. For example, instead of saying, *You look great in that outfit*, say something like *Seeing you smile in that photo makes me smile. I love when you are happy!* Maybe instead of saying, *Have fun* when looking at someone's vacation photos, you say something like *You deserve to have fun because you're always so kind to people.* Notice if you, too, see an increase in the positive comments you receive, because quite often, the more you give, the more you receive! If you are not using social media, find another way, such as giving a personal compliment, sending a text, etc. Try to do this activity for seven days straight and evaluate the results you see at the end of the week.

Compliment Cards

In the past, you may have used construction paper and crayons to create cards to celebrate people's birthdays or other holidays. If you have been going through a rough patch with someone, try creating a card for them filled with compliments to celebrate the positives. Thank them for whatever good things they bring to your life. Be creative and use paints, markers, or whatever artistic material you have on hand, or send an e-card. You can also create compliment cards to give to people who may be feeling down or going through a rough time. Receiving the card will help add to someone's joy, and when you see that it has made them happy, you'll be happy too!

Loving Lyrics

Using loving lyrics from songs can help to add light and positive energy to situations where friends and family are not seeing the good in themselves. For example, if a friend is nervous and thinking their presentation in English class will be terrible, try singing or playing a few lines from Katy Perry's song "Firework." If your sister is worried about what she's going to wear to a party, make sure she knows how beautiful you think she is and sing or play a song like Bruno Mars's "Just the Way You Are." If you have a friend struggling because someone said something nasty to them, try playing or singing a couple of lines from a song like Taylor Swift's "Shake It Off."

Unsung Hero Checklist

Create a weekly checklist for yourself, setting positive goals where you look for the good in the everyday heroes in your life and offer them praise for their positives. List people you typically don't interact with. Consider people such as the cafeteria workers who make your lunch every day or the custodian who ensures that your classes are clean. These are the unsung heroes who allow you to function and live your life, but who often do not receive credit or recognition for what they do. Offer these people a verbal thank you when you see them for all they do. For example, thank the custodian for the way the floors always sparkle in the gym, or let the cafeteria worker know how great the yogurt parfaits always taste. If you look, you'll find lots of unsung heroes at school and at home too. Make sure you check off your accomplishments on your list for the week, and keep track of your progress toward your goal of celebrating these unsung heroes and thanking them for their service.

Affirmation: I am excellent at seeing the good in myself and others.

> *Look for the good, look for the good. Life sure would be sweeter if everybody would.*
> —Jason Mraz

PART FOUR: HEALTHY ENGAGEMENT WITH THE WORLD

Chapter 14: Mindful Meaning Making

Life is without meaning. You bring the meaning to it.
—Joseph Campbell

Affirmation: The meaning I bring to my life is beautiful and empowering.

Jessica's Story

Jessica's English teacher, Mrs. Jones, gave her an opportunity to earn extra credit by completing an additional writing assignment. She loved scripted television and decided to write a letter to a TV network pitching an idea for a show. She spent several weeks working on this letter, feeling incredibly inspired. She grew more and more excited about it the more she worked on it. She submitted it to her teacher with pride, believing she would get an A+. She planned to submit it to a network one day. This project really lit her up, and she couldn't wait to hear what her teacher had to say. The following week she stayed after class to get the teacher's feedback. The teacher asked her a few questions about her ideas and made some suggestions. She then handed Jessica the paper with a B at the top, along with a lot of red writing and more questions and suggestions along the sides of the paper.

Jessica left the classroom feeling crushed, with tears in her eyes. As she walked down the hallway, she began to cry. Mrs. Jones must have really hated her writing to give her a B. Suddenly she felt a tap on the shoulder. It was her friend Gigi. Gigi asked her if she was okay. All Jessica could do was hand the paper with the red B over to Gigi. Gigi looked at the paper and said, "Wow! You got a B from Mrs. Jones? That's great!"

Jessica was shocked for a minute. She had felt ashamed and embarrassed, but what Gigi said made her rethink her reaction. That B made her feel like she was a bad writer, but Gigi thought a B was great. When Jessica thought about it, Mrs. Jones never actually said she was stupid or that her writing was bad. She simply gave her suggestions on how to improve what she'd written. Jessica realized she had made her teacher's feedback mean that her writing was terrible. Her teacher didn't say those things at all! So why was Jessica creating that story? She realized how much her own thoughts were upsetting her. She pointed this out to herself and started to question why her mind went to such a negative place. It helped her feel better to observe the stories and question them. She noticed that the negative emotion was lifted by this awareness.

Why You Should Mindfully Make Meaning

We give things meaning in order to understand and make sense of our world. It is possible to control our thoughts before they become negative and lead us in the wrong direction. We are literally inventing our own reality with the stories we tell ourselves. Our mind's stories can potentially keep us from thinking positively, produce anxiety, contribute to procrastination, and stop us from taking risks. The behavior of making up false or negative stories can prevent us from living to our full potential! For example, Jessica could have chosen to never write again. Jessica could have allowed that inaccurate story she created in her mind, thinking she was a bad writer, to keep her from going after her dreams. If we don't notice or question when our thoughts become negative, they can keep us from feeling the way we want to feel, acting the way we want to act, and living the way we want to live. Once we have awareness, we can shift and change our perceived stories to create a new and positive reality.

Ways to Mindfully Make Meaning

Construct Positive Constructs

For this activity, you will need three stackable items such as blocks, cans, and old boxes; sticky notes (or small pieces of paper and tape); and a marker or pen. Constructs are ideas we have that are not based on evidence. On a sticky note, write a negative idea (construct) you have about yourself that you feel you have the power to change. This could include ideas like *I am lazy* or *I am a terrible speller.* On another sticky note, turn your negative construct into a positive one. For example, *I am becoming more active with daily exercise*, or *My spelling has improved because I am reading for pleasure.*

Do this with a few constructs you are looking to improve. Stick your negative construct on one side of a stackable item and your positive construct on the other side of the same item. Do this for your three constructs and put your items one on top of another so they make a tower. Make sure the negative constructs are facing you. Look at them for a moment and release them in your mind, saying goodbye as you knock down the tower and the negative constructs. Now, rebuild your tower with the positive constructs facing you. Take a moment to reread your positive constructs. Once you are finished, take the positive sticky notes and post them somewhere to maintain your focus on the positive for your future.

High Cue

A haiku is a Japanese poem containing a total of seventeen syllables in three lines. The first line has five syllables, the second line has seven syllables, and the third line has five syllables. In this activity, you'll write a haiku that helps to lift your spirits higher and reminds you (or cues you) about some of the great things about you. This will help you create a positive picture of yourself. If you are unsure how many syllables are in a word, search the internet, using the words *syllable counter* for assistance. Use your first name as the title of your haiku. When you need to avoid negative thinking and stop yourself from obsessing over things that may not be true, reread it. Notice how you feel after you have read the haiku. Hang the poem where it will remind you of your wonderful qualities. Here is an example:

Hunter
Loyal friend to all (five syllables)
Makes others laugh profusely (seven syllables)
Super caring guy (five syllables)

Color Your Thoughts

It is very easy to let our thoughts take us down a dark road. Instead of keeping thoughts positive and bright when we review situations or interactions with people, we sometimes see only the worst parts of those experiences. The next time your thoughts are leading you down the dark path, grab a coloring book and crayons, pick the brightest colors you can, and start coloring. You can purchase crayons cheaply at local dollar stores. Be sure to choose something that makes you happy. You can also search the internet for *coloring pages* and print out images you find online. With each stroke of bright color, try to create more positive thoughts, and look on the brighter side of the situation. Imagine your thoughts lightening and turning happy and peaceful. Hang up or save your drawing, and look at it the next time you need to shift your thinking.

Neutralize Negativity

Earthing, sometimes known as grounding, is the action of walking barefoot outdoors. Scientific research shows that this process is known to generate negative ions to neutralize the body, which can calm your nervous system. Speak with your parents to determine if you have a safe place to do this. You'll want a place that is free from sharp objects, things like fire ants and bees, and hard rocks.

If you do have a safe place, consider going outside and

walking around barefoot the next time your mind starts to tell you stories that aren't true. Approximately thirty minutes of grounding or earthing is said to have health benefits. Pairing it with the idea of letting go of your negative thinking can be even more beneficial. If earthing is not an option, consider using a Himalayan salt lamp or an essential oil diffuser to neutralize your negative thinking and create a more balanced thought process.

Feeling Boarding

For this activity, you will need scissors, glue, old magazines, and a piece of cardboard or poster board. You may have heard of creating a vision board where you cut out pictures of what you would like to see in your future. For this variation, think of some positive emotions you want to invite into your life. For example, emotions like joy, accomplishment, peace, safety, and love.

Using images and words, create a board that inspires the feelings you want to have in your future. For example, if one of your words is *peaceful*, you could cut out a picture of a beach and/or the word *peace*. Invite the words into your mind that the pictures help you experience. For example, if the ocean in the picture helps you to feel joy, feel it! Imagine all the sensations, including sitting in the beach chair hearing the relaxing waves, smelling the salt air, and feeling the sand under your feet. Hang your feeling board somewhere you can regularly use it to experience all those good feelings it helps bring to mind.

Vision Writing

Grab a piece of paper and think of something you want in your life. For example, wonderful friends, to feel good in your body, good grades, or a better relationship with your parents. Take a moment to visualize how you would like your future to look. Now write about something as if it has already happened. For example, if you're struggling with skin issues, you could write, *I am so happy to feel comfortable and confident in my body. I love how beautiful my skin looks—it's absolutely glowing! My skin is 100 percent clear, and the acne will never return. I'm so proud of myself for eating healthy and practicing self-care. I have a healthy relationship with my body, and it feels so good. I love my body and myself more than I ever have.* Write the current date on the top of the paper. Keep this statement somewhere close, and repeat it to yourself multiple times a day. Notice what happens in your life, and watch your progress from that day on.

Catching the Monster in Meaning Making

In conversation with an adult or someone you trust, share an experience that led you to think negatively about yourself. For example, "My partner broke up with me and led me to think I was not good enough or something was wrong with me." Talk about the monster you made of the meaning and how you can shift your thinking in a positive direction, and ask yourself if the meaning you made is actually accurate. In this example, is it true that you are not good enough or something is wrong with you?

If you are having difficulty seeing the other side of the story and challenging your thoughts, work with the adult you trust to understand this better. In the future, you can catch the monster in your meaning making. Observe how your mind is working, and question your thinking. Remember all your positive attributes and good qualities. If you find yourself creating monsters in your meaning making in the future, reach out to an adult or someone you trust.

The Mental STOP Sign

When you catch yourself thinking negatively, visualize a STOP sign. In this case, stop and think. *Is what I'm thinking helping me or hurting me? Is the thought hurting someone or helping someone else?* Practice visualizing the STOP sign each time you are thinking negatively, and ask yourself these questions. Pay attention to the subtle shift you feel in your mood. If you find that a thought hurts you or someone else, then it's a negative thought, and it's time to replace it with a positive one. The more you practice using this mental STOP sign, the more it will help you develop a positive mindset. For example, Mike was on his way to school thinking, *I don't want to go to school today.* He paused, visualized the STOP sign, and asked if the thought was helping or hurting. His thought was not actually harmful or hurtful, but if he acted upon his negative thought and stayed home, he knew it would hurt his grades and actually have consequences. He thought about what to replace the negative thought with and came up with a positive thought: *If I keep my grades up, I will graduate with my friends.* Continue to practice looking for the good in situations, and you will create more rewarding experiences.

Affirmation: I have the power to change the stories my mind creates.

It is only a thought and a thought can be changed.
—Louise Hay

Chapter 15: Eat for Wellness

*The food you eat can be either the safest and most powerful
form of medicine or the slowest form of poison.*
—Ann Wigmore

Affirmation: My healthy eating choices enhance my physical and
emotional health.

Patrick's Story

Patrick was diagnosed with leukemia in 2016. At that time, he
was fatigued most of the time and had significant pain in parts
of his body. For the first six months, Patrick was just trying to
comprehend what leukemia was, what he could do about it, and if
there was something he did to manifest this illness. After a great
deal of reflection, some things became clear to him. He started to
see how negative thinking, high stress levels, and poor diet may
have contributed to his situation.

Since he was still learning about the many natural ways
that he could help heal cancer, the first thing he did was radically
change his eating habits to a mostly whole foods and plant-based
diet. He removed meat, sugar, dairy, processed foods, and some
wheat from his meals. These changes were based on the research
and stories found in the book *Radical Remission: Surviving Cancer
Against All Odds* by Dr. Kelly Turner. Changing his eating habits
was an action step that was completely within his control. The
results were incredibly positive, which made the transition from
a Standard American Diet (SAD) to a whole-food and plant-based
one easy to maintain. Patrick lost about thirty pounds, his energy
returned, and his blood counts started to stabilize. The results
kept him highly motivated. Patrick knew that he had to change

his diet in order to save his life. That was his first step in dealing with a diagnosis of cancer. If you were to take anything away from Patrick's story, it would be to know that food is one of the best medicines.

Why Eat for Wellness?

Part of your overall health and wellness depends on good nutrition. What you eat can be considered a foundation of your success. In the above story, food was Patrick's medicine. Food is also chemistry. That is why some foods work in our bodies and other foods do not. Healthy food fuels our bodies and increases our energy, keeping us motivated. Making good food choices also boosts our immune system.

Healthy eating can be a very confusing topic. There is a variety of research, opinions, and beliefs about what constitutes a healthy diet. Healthy eating is different for everyone, and you will need to determine what meets your individual needs. Cancer or chronic illness doesn't have to be your motivation to make changes. Self-medicating or overeating unhealthy foods can lead to issues such as obesity, depression, tooth decay, headaches, high blood pressure, high cholesterol, skin conditions, heart disease, stroke, diabetes, eating disorders, and inflammation. Managing your weight, maintaining a strong immune system, and reducing chronic illness are the results of eating for wellness. Healthy eating reduces trips to the doctor and the need for medications, and it can increase your lifespan. If you practice prevention while you're young, you will look and feel better when you're older.

How to Learn to Eat for Wellness

Movie Time

With your parent or guardian's permission, watch one of the following documentaries: *Super Size Me*; *Forks Over Knives*; *Food, Inc.*; *Food Matters*; *Fat, Sick & Nearly Dead*; *Hungry for Change*; *Dirt! The Movie*; *May I Be Frank*; *Killer At Large*; *Cowspiracy*; *(UN)well*; or *What the Health*. Most of these can be found on Netflix and

Amazon. If you do not have access to these services, use YouTube to search for clips from the movies to watch. (Content warning: Some of these films contain depictions of animal mistreatment that could be upsetting for some viewers.) Share some of the information that you learned with family or friends. Think about and discuss how you can implement what you have learned from these videos into your own personal life or food choices.

Label Learning

Pick your favorite snack with a label and look at the ingredients. If the item does not have the ingredients on the label, look them up online. How many ingredients were you familiar with? How many did you need to look up? How many ingredients surprised or concerned you? If you are now thinking that this snack may not be the best option, search online for a healthier alternative. Find something that has a shorter list of ingredients that still tastes good. For example, you may have determined your granola bar has high fructose corn syrup, sugar, palm kernel oil, fructose, maltodextrin, salt, soy lecithin, and mixed tocopherols. After researching, you can find an alternative granola bar that may also be organic and contains only oats, egg whites, almonds, cashews, and dates.

Dirty Dozen/Clean 15

The Environmental Working Group (EWG) provides resources and conducts research that helps to protect you in many ways. This group of people updates two lists every year: *The Dirty Dozen* and *The Clean 15*. *The Dirty Dozen* is a list of the fruits and vegetables that are most heavily sprayed with pesticides. *The Clean 15* is a list of foods that are least sprayed or affected by pesticides. The EWG encourages purchasing organic foods if they are on *The Dirty Dozen* list, while they consider it safer to eat non-organically if they are on *The Clean 15* list. Go to their website (ewg.org) and print or save the newest version of these lists. Consider bringing this list with you next time you go food shopping or sharing your list with your parents or guardian.

Cafeteria Challenge

Consider what your school cafeteria is serving for lunch. What ingredients are part of the meal? For example, if your cafeteria is serving ham sandwiches, does the ham contain possibly harmful chemicals that should be avoided? Are there items on the menu that you feel you could make healthier versions of? Try redesigning a recipe for one. Be sure to include the ingredients and the steps involved, and try making the new recipe yourself at home if possible. Consider talking with the person who runs the cafeteria about your revised version of the menu item to determine if it's something that could be substituted in the future.

Cookbook Creating

Research healthy recipes that you think you and your family will enjoy. Write your own cookbook and include recipes and photos of the meals. You can include healthy versions of your family's cultural dishes. Try to include vegetables or fruits in all the dishes you are selecting. For example, if you like brownies, use beets in the batter. If your family loves lasagna, try replacing the noodles with eggplant and zucchini. Once you've completed your cookbook, consider having it printed professionally and giving it as a gift to a parent or family member.

Sugar-Coated Crossword

There are over fifty different names for sugar in our food. A few examples include high fructose corn syrup, sucrose, glucose, fructose, lactose, maltodextrin, and dextrose. Find a website that will help you create your own word search for all these various names for sugar. Enter the words into the site to create your word search puzzle, using as many names for sugar as possible. Once you're done, dare a family member or friend to find all the names and complete the word search.

FDA Read the Label

Search the internet for *FDA Read the Label.* The FDA stands for Food and Drug Administration, and on their website, you'll find activities and videos that can help you gain a better understanding of how to read labels and understand ingredients. Have fun exploring this website. Select an activity or as many as you would like to complete. Try to share this link with at least five other friends or family members.

Affirmation: I am loving myself by eating nourishing food.

The food you eat is as important as the thoughts you think.
—Louise Hay

Chapter 16: Sustain the Planet

Climate change is the single greatest threat to a sustainable future but, at the same time, addressing the climate challenge presents a golden opportunity to promote prosperity, security and a brighter future for all.
—Ban Ki-Moon, Former Secretary-General of the United Nations

Affirmation: I can make the greatest change to help preserve and protect the environment that surrounds me.

Lois's Story

Lois was scanning through YouTube and watched a video on Greta Thunberg, a twenty-year-old girl who's made a significant difference toward addressing climate change. Greta became a vegan when she was eight years old and started a movement called Fridays for Future, inspiring hundreds of thousands of students around the world to stand up for the environment. Since then, she'd spoken publicly in many countries, traveling in zero-emission vehicles and explaining that economic growth without sustainability in mind was not the way to a sustainable future. She also wrote a book called *The Climate Book: Facts and Solutions*. Her superpower, inspiring others with words and writing about the things that were most important to her, had made a significant impact.

Lois decided to get together with a group of friends and start her own movement, just as Greta had done. The group met regularly to discuss how they could spread awareness locally and educate people about improving their environment. They even presented to the board of education at school to gain more support for changing the school's curriculum and policies. They hoped that these policy changes would make systemic and long-lasting change for the next group of students entering the school. In addition, they knew the changes could have a ripple effect and impact the community positively.

In essence, the school became the epicenter of sustainability efforts and positive change in their area on behalf of the environment. Her group gained the support of the local PTA and other political organizations and began running educational green fairs in the community. Lois was eventually appointed as an honorary member to the board of education, as a spokesperson for sustainability. Eventually, their work did impact school policies regarding the use of green cleaning supplies, clean energy in the school, and implementing an aquaponics program, which resulted in sustainable food for the cafeteria. Lois was inspired by Greta Thunberg, and many of her peers are also becoming activists for a sustainable future.

Why Sustain the Planet?

Numerous studies have shown the ways in which humans are contributing to climate. There are many environmental movements today that seek not only to sustain but to repair and restore the damage humans have caused and that encourage people to work together with the planet to ensure our impact is healthy and balanced. It is critical to learn the science about climate change and what it takes to make a difference to preserve and protect our planet. Many of the activities in this book relate to your emotional and physical health. Getting involved in helping to sustain the only planet we have is a great way to feel good about yourself by doing something sustainable for others.

The world needs more leaders to take charge and make changes. Consider Greta Thunberg's activism and what she accomplished. Greta started at home, and so can you. Small steps can be taken right in your own home and in your community to make a big difference. Taking on a task such as inspiring school leaders to make sustainable changes is a step on the path to sustainability. You can encourage your school to develop curriculum, to learn about climate change, and to take action. You can present solutions to the public regarding the environmental interests of the community by learning the facts, becoming aware, and speaking your mind. You can pursue opportunities to learn about technical or college pathways that will lead you to a career in the environmental sector, also called a green-collar career. If you are looking to volunteer, keep in mind that you can be part of the solution and contribute to a healthier, sustainable, and regenerative planet.

How to Start Sustaining the Planet

Energy Enlightenment

Many local energy companies offer free assessments and information regarding the performance of your home's energy consumption in comparison to other homes like yours. Work with your parents or guardians to get a copy of this information from the energy company that serves your home. If your home is not performing well, work with your parents or guardians to analyze what can be changed to reduce your energy consumption and costs.

Can you change traditional light bulbs to LED? Can you switch to washing laundry using cold water instead of warm? You can apply this to other areas related to the environment or conserving resources. Can you change your shower head to one that uses less water? Consider all the possibilities, within reason, that might be options for you and your family.

If you are unable to do this, you may want to conduct a climate change audit in your own town. Look for things that are unsustainable and may be contributing to climate change. Your audit can be in the areas of energy production and use, transportation, waste management, educational programs that teach people about sustainability, or food choices being made and products being purchased in your community that are not sustainable. Make a list of items that can be improved and decide how and to whom you will present your findings.

Environmental PSA

Create a positive public service announcement (PSA) about the environment that will reach people of all ages in your community. Once you determine your message, summarize all the important details to create a short speech that is under three minutes and a slide show presentation detailing your concerns about your local community. Consider working with your school's science teacher or principal to attend a local board of education meeting to share your thoughts and concerns. Ask the board members if they have plans to create a healthier learning environment at lower operational cost. Additionally, you can ask them if they have a sustainability policy for the district. This may spark ongoing conversations and lead to change in your school or community.

Captain Eco

Interview a friend, a family member, or a community member to see what strategies they are currently using to contribute to a healthier environment. Use what you learn to design a climate change character who has a superpower that can change the environment. Create a comic or storyboard that shows the superpower and character in action.

Time Warp

Imagine being transported to 2050, into a world where we have all taken positive steps toward conservation and protection of the earth and its natural resources. Develop a fictional podcast where you are interviewed by a friend, and you discuss all of the positive steps that have been taken to do this. What have people accomplished? Are all houses powered by solar energy? Have the oceans been cleaned, and are they free of trash? Are large cities free of pollution because factories have found ways to limit their emissions and protect the atmosphere? There are endless possibilities regarding what you can imagine for the future. Listen to your podcast and consider what steps you can take right now in your own life to create a healthy earth.

Mission Green-Collar Career

Your mission, if you choose to accept it, is to research green-collar careers and find a way to share what you've learned with your family, school community, and guidance counselors. You can do this by investigating websites such as the US Bureau of Labor Statistics (BLS) to learn about the outlook for environmental careers. There will be increases in the job market and demand for these careers in coming years. Employment websites such as Indeed will give you information on salaries and the qualifications and education required for different roles. Socially responsible companies will require employees to be knowledgeable about sustainability.

Design a campaign to share what you've learned with your target audience. You can do this by creating a brochure, a website, a video, a rap song, or other types of graphics to promote green-collar careers and environmental awareness.

Green Art

Create some form of green art that addresses the importance of regenerating and protecting the environment. You can write a poem, design window art in your home that communicates positive messages, compose a song about environmental sustainability, or create an illustration of the song's lyrics. You can also design a museum art piece that you've created from recycled objects, create a playlist of favorite songs with environmental themes, or write a one-act play that can be performed in your school about the environment. Don't be afraid to express your feelings through your art about this topic you are passionate about. Consider sharing your artwork on social media or with friends, family, and your community.

Affirmation: I am protecting my future when I help sustain the planet.

> *Preserve and cherish the pale blue dot, the*
> *only home we've ever known.*
> —Carl Sagan

CONCLUSION

Now that you have taken your empower trip, you possess a set of tools to assist you on your path to the future. You can decide how you respond to every situation you encounter, even during challenging times. You can refer to any of the activities we have provided and revisit the tools when issues come up in your life. Even challenging experiences can be incredibly rewarding, like training for a tough sport. As your empower trip has shown you, you have the power to move toward something wonderful despite (or sometimes because of) the challenges. Your power comes from within, and applying it is the path to self-love and love for others. When you love yourself, you gain confidence, take risks, fully express yourself, and feel happier. When you love others, you have strong connections and bonds and a support system that is there for you and allows for happiness.

There are so many ways to empower yourself. Do what truly brings you joy, give love to your mind and body, and put yourself first. You can trust that things will work out even when you're full of doubt. Don't allow fear to stop you from taking risks. Be unapologetically you! You can also say no to something that makes you feel uncomfortable, forgive yourself and others, practice gratitude, and find perfection in your imperfections. Taking back your power is a wonderful feeling.

If you have the intention and the tools to be empowered, you can feel worthy and live life from a place of strength. Your life is essentially a storybook with many different chapters, and you have the power to craft each and every page. Your strength comes from believing that you can create new opportunities and great memories, today and every day. Be patient, and know that tomorrow is a brand-new day with new beginnings. Believe that you have enormous potential. You have it in you to do great things. You are and always will be a beautiful shining light. You truly are a star.

RESOURCES

Click on our QR code below to access additional *Empower Trip* resources:

BIBLIOGRAPHY

Alter, Charlotte, Suyin Haynes, and Justin Worland. "Time 2019 Person of the Year: Greta Thunberg." *Time*, December 23/ December 30, 2019. https://time.com/person-of-the-year-2019-greta-thunberg/.

American Psychological Association. "Stress in America: Our Health at Risk." APA.org. January 11, 2012. https://www.apa.org/news/press/releases/stress/2011/final-2011.pdf.

Beecher, H. K. "The Powerful Placebo." *JAMA* 159, no. 17 (December 24, 1955): 1602–6.

Bumbaca, Chris. "Saint Peter's March Madness Run Has Made Guard Doug Edert 'Folk Hero with a Mustache.'" *USA Today*. March 25, 2022. https://www.usatoday.com/story/sports/ncaab/2022/03/25/saint-peters-doug-edert-mustache-2022-march-madness/7155207001/.

Ding-Edwards, Laura. *The Mountain.* Liverpool, England: That Guy's House, 2019.

Erle, Thorsten M., and Sascha Topolinski. "The Grounded Nature of Psychological Perspective-taking." *Journal of Personality and Social Psychology* 112, no. 5 (2017): 683–695.

EWG Science Team. "EWG 2023 Shopper's Guide to Pesticides in Produce." The Environmental Working Group. March 15, 2023. https://www.ewg.org/foodnews/summary.php.

Gallo, Carmine. "The Maya Angelou Quote That Will Radically Improve Your Business." *Forbes*, May 1, 2014. https://www.forbes.com/sites/carminegallo/2014/05/31/the-maya-angelou-quote-that-will-radically-improve-your-business/?sh=22cbfc82118b.

Gray, John. *Men Are from Mars, Women Are from Venus: A Practical Guide for Improving Communication and Getting What You Want in Your Relationships.* New York, NY: HarperCollins Publishers, 1992.

Hay, Louise L. *You Can Heal Your Life.* Carlsbad, California: Hay House, 1999.

Hoffman, Adam. "Can Negative Thinking Actually Make You Sick?" *Health*, January 4, 2023. https://www.health.com/condition/heart-disease/can-negative-thinking-make-you-sick#:~:text=You%20may%20know%20that%20stress,health%20problems%2C%20like%20heart%20disease.

Intergovernmental Panel on Climate Change. "Climate Change 2023 Synthesis Report." IPCC. n.d. https://www.ipcc.ch/report/ar6/syr/.

Jeffers, Susan. *Feel the Fear and Do It Anyway.* London, England: Vermilion, 2007.

Marchant, Jo. "How Happiness Boosts the Immune System." *Scientific American*, November 27, 2013. https://www.scientificamerican.com/article/how-happiness-boosts-the-immune-system/.

Mayo Clinic Staff. "Chronic Stress Puts Your Health at Risk." The Mayo Clinic. August 1, 2023. https://www.mayoclinic.org/healthy-lifestyle/stress-management/in-depth/stress/art-20046037.

Melrose, Regalena. *The 60 Seconds Fix: The Brain Changing Toolkit that Stops Unwanted Habits and Starts Surprising Joy*. Long Beach, California: 60 Seconds Press, 2013.

National Center for Complementary and Integrated Health. "Meditation and Mindfulness: What You Need to Know." US Department of Health and Human Services. June 2022. https://www.nccih.nih.gov/health/meditation-and-mindfulness-what-you-need-to-know.

Ruder, Debra Bradley. "The Enteric Nervous System That Regulates Our Gut Is Often Called the Body's 'Second Brain.'" Harvard Medical School. Winter 2017. https://hms.harvard.edu/news-events/publications-archive/brain/gut-brain.

Sotera Wireless. "National Stress Awareness Day—November 3." Sotera Digital Health. November 3, 2021. https://soteradigitalhealth.com/events/national-stress-awareness-day-november-3#:~:text=November%203%2C%202021,Day%20%2D%20November%203.

Turner, Kelly. *Radical Remission: Surviving Cancer against All Odds.* New York: HarperCollins Publishers, 2018.

Turner, Kelly. *Radical Hope: 10 Key Healing Factors from Exceptional Survivors of Cancer and Other Diseases.* Carlsbad, California: Hay House, 2020.

Yugay, Irina. "Why 'Earthing' Is the Ultimate Biohack—and How to Do It Today." Mindvalley. November 2, 2022. https://blog.mindvalley.com/earthing/#:~:text=Scientific%20tests%20and%20research%20suggest,at%20one%20hour%20per%20day.

ACKNOWLEDGEMENTS

The authors would like to thank Lindsey Alexander and editorial staff from The Reading List; Penny Fisher, holistic practitioner, former school administrator and teacher; Gordon Fisher, holistic practitioner, former teacher; Patricia Hice, reader and former assessor; Kelly Turner, PhD, *New York Times* bestselling author of *Radical Remission: Surviving Cancer against All Odds;* the Institute for Integrative Nutrition; and especially our families, friends, and colleagues who have offered ongoing support and insight.

ABOUT THE AUTHORS

Kim Weiler has enjoyed a long career working in all facets of the television and film industry. With over twenty-five years of experience, she has worked both in front of the camera and behind the scenes. For the last seventeen years, she has served as a production accountant on dozens of documentaries, feature films, and unscripted series. She is a proud member of the Producers Guild of America. She devotes her spare time to teaching others about empowerment and self-love and is the author of the book *PS —It's All About Love: How A Painful Journey with Psoriasis Became a Life Devoted to Helping Others.* Additionally, Kim is a motivational speaker and founder of The Love Group, a nonprofit organization whose mission is to empower our youth. She has learned from experience that feeling good about ourselves, with all of our human imperfections, is the key to living a fulfilling life. You can learn more at www.kimweiler.com. She currently lives in North Carolina with her husband, mother, and her pup, Cora.

Dana Hice DePugh has over thirty years of experience in education and has served as an assistant superintendent for nine years, teacher, learning disabilities consultant, and supervisor. She is a former school board member and president and has served as the project director for and author of numerous grants. She was instrumental in starting a number of innovative special education, early childhood, and career and technical programs. With undergraduate degrees in Education and Psychology, a masters in Special Education, a masters in Metaphysical Science, and a PhD in Metaphysical Counseling, she now combines her educational experience with holistic healing methodologies and energy medicine, serving as the CEO for The Mind Fairy, LLC. She currently teaches meditation and alternative healing to clients. Her personal hobbies include cooking, gardening, and spending time designing and creating wood art with her husband, Eric.

John Henry has worked for over twenty-nine years in public education. With a masters in Technology Education, he coordinated and coauthored an electric vehicle program during his teaching career that received a NASA Explorer Schools grant. He was selected as a NASA Einstein Fellow, serving at NASA's Office of Education. He later joined the New Jersey School Boards Association as senior manager of Science, Technology, Engineering, Arts, and Mathematics (STEAM) and Sustainable Schools. He collaborated with the US Army to develop outreach, leadership, and team-building programs for high school students. He was lead trainer for a Federal Department of Education grant in Technology and Problem-Based Learning. He served on the board of directors for the US Green Building Council and managed New Jersey's Green Program of Study for the NJ Department of Education. He has received awards and recognition from Sustainable Jersey, NJ Audubon, and the Department of Environmental Protection. John is a leukemia survivor and is currently helping others on their journeys with cancer. He is a certified Radical Remission instructor and a holistic health and wellness coach. His resilience and well-being come from vulnerability, relaxation, and acceptance. He has three children and enjoys hiking, cooking, gardening, and spending time with his friends at the New Jersey Shore.

Printed in Great Britain
by Amazon

30260146R00074